From Country to Suburb

The Development of the Bexley Area from 1800 to the present day

by
Malcolm Barr-Hamilton
and
Leonard Reilly

Bexley London Borough
Leisure Services Department
1996

Published 1996

British Library Cataloguing in Publication Data.
A catalogue record for this book is available
from the British Library

Bexley Leisure Services Department
Local Studies Centre
Hall Place, Bourne Road
Bexley, Kent DA5 1PQ

ISBN 0 902541 34X

Designed by Bexley London Borough Graphic Studio

BEXLEY
COUNCIL

J.

Contents

Country to Suburb

Part of the first Ordnance Survey map of Kent, published in 1801. It shows the borough's area as almost totally rural; small villages and hamlets separated by large areas of fields interspersed with substantial areas of ancient wood and wild heathland.

Introduction

Two hundred years ago the area now known as Bexley London Borough was open countryside: farmland, woodland, heathland and parkland. For administrative purposes it was divided into six parishes, each with its own parish church, namely Bexley, Crayford, East Wickham, Erith, Footscray and North Cray. Much of the population of some 4,200 people was concentrated in the long-established villages of Bexley, Crayford, Erith, East Wickham, Footscray, North Cray and Welling, while others lived in scattered farmsteads and hamlets such as Bridgen, Upton, Picardy, Blackfen and Northend.

The district, like others on the fringe of London, was well endowed with country houses some with extensive and growing estates such as Hall Place, Danson, Footscray Place and Belvedere.

The first change to this long-established pattern came early in the nineteenth century with the enclosure of Bexley Heath by Acts of Parliament in 1812 and 1814, and the subsequent establishment of what at first was known as Bexley New Town and later as the town of Bexleyheath. A precursor to further change was the construction of the North Kent Railway, completed in 1849. This was a significant factor in the transformation of Erith from a riverside village to an important industrial town by the end of the century and the establishment of a new semi-suburban village called Belvedere.

Similarly, the opening of the Dartford Loop Line in 1866 contributed to the changing face of Bexley Village and the transformation of Sidcup over the course of forty years from a hamlet into a sizeable town. By the end of the nineteenth century the population of what is now Bexley London Borough stood at approximately 54,000.

Growth continued in the early years of the twentieth century. The arrival of electric tramways providing cheap and reliable transport to the Thameside industrial areas of Erith and Woolwich further facilitated development at Welling, Bexleyheath and Northumberland Heath. The First World War brought further development, especially to Crayford, Erith and Welling, where housing was required for the massive influx of munitions workers.

In the 1920s a new phase of development was entered as the old landed estates such as that of Danson started to be broken up and the Housing Acts of 1923 and 1924 stimulated council house building in the district. However, by 1930 the district was still predominantly rural; but this was to change dramatically in the next decade. A variety of causes including electrification of the railways, road building, failure of agriculture, and the availability of government housing subsidies, led to development on an unprecedented scale. Fields vanished with amazing rapidity making way for semi-detached houses and bungalows. Whole new communities were established such as at Albany Park and Falconwood with their own new railway stations, shopping parades and pubs. Within a few years the district was transformed into a metropolitan suburb.

Introduction

Suburban growth continued after World War Two but on a much more limited scale. Some of the largest developments have been council estates such as the Bedensfield Estate developed by the Chislehurst and Sidcup Urban District Council at North Cray in the late 1950s. Since the 1960s development has been characterised by infill - the building on pieces of land not used in the inter-war boom or redevelopment of large Victorian properties, notably in Belvedere, Bexley and Sidcup.

Without doubt, the greatest development since the war has been the creation of the new town of Thamesmead straddling the Boroughs of Bexley and Greenwich.

This book is based on the exhibition of the same title which was on show in Hall Place during the Summer of 1995. It has been compiled using the collections of Bexley's Local Studies Centre.

Although some of the pictures have been included in earlier publications we feel their quality justifies their further reproduction. The majority have never been published before.
The book shows only a tiny fraction of the many thousands of illustrations held by the borough. Also available are books, pamphlets, old newspapers, ephemera and maps. These along with the archival records of the area tell the story of Bexley's past.

We are grateful to the following for granting permission to reproduce their photographs: Museum of London, p. 14; Aerofilms, p. 47, 60, 80; the John Topham Picture Library, p. 9, 10, 49, 65, 66, 75, 76, 81; Kentish Times Newspapers, p. 82, 83, 84; Greenwich Local History Library, p. 4.

Finally we would like to thank all those people who have given invaluable assistance in the production of both the original exhibition and this book; Sue Barclay, Janet Benton, Lilian Booker, Frances Sweeny, Jessica Vale, Carole Whybrow, Keith Turnbull Photography, and Richard Meek and the staff of Bexley London Borough's Graphics Studio, especially John Hunter.

Agriculture

Bexley's agricultural past is still within living memory; it is a past that diminished greatly in the building boom of the 1930s but which still survives in part even today. These survivals are in the form of remaining farmland particularly in the North Cray area, buildings and objects (such as the granary from Manor Farm, Bexley, re-erected near Hall Place) and redundant farming equipment in the collections of Bexley Museums, some of which are displayed during the summer months in the Hall Place Visitor Centre.

Not all land in the Bexley area has been suited to agriculture as there were large acres of poorly drained riverside marshes, woodland and on Bexley Heath, wild open heath land similar in character to Dartford Heath today. It was principally the expansion of London in the 17th and 18th centuries and the disappearance of farmland in the new inner suburbs of Bermondsey and Deptford that put pressure on local landowners to farm more intensively. Woodland was felled, principally the almost 400-acre West

Tanyard Farm which was located to the west of Bexley Park Wood, in about 1900. It was farmed by the Watkins family, who remained there until 1934. The River Shuttle flows under the bridge in the foreground.

Agriculture

A heavily laden cart of cabbages at Bruce Gibson's Farm, East Wickham. The pond was next to the house on the west side of Wickham Street and the farm area includes the present East Wickham open space.

Wood to the north of Blackfen Road and the heath land of Bexley Heath enclosed. This growth of London and the arrival of the railways enabled many local farmers to endure the farming depression of the last quarter of the 19th century.

As the landscape changed during the 19th century so, at least in part, did produce and methods. Grain and animal husbandry were superseded by vegetables, market gardening, and fruit and flower nurseries.

A busy scene of hop pickers in Sidcup c.1912. The location is unknown. Note in particular the young age of those at work and the number of very young children. Note also the women's heavy clothing, uncomfortable in the summer heat, and the drink bottles necessary for refreshment in the long working day.

The new crop with the widest social effects was the hop. Hops were grown at Hurst, Tanyard, Days Lane, Ruxley and Halfway Street Farms and September saw an influx of Londoners for the picking season .

Two of the most notable farming families at the end of the last century were the Vinsons, fruit specialists, who worked the farms named above along with others in Bexley and Bexleyheath and further out to the south east; and the Gibsons who farmed extensively at East Wickham.

Ploughing at Ruxley Farm in 1939.

Agriculture

The arrival of the railways and in particular the Bexleyheath line in 1895 saw an increase in soft fruit and flower production. Predominant along with the Vinsons were the Ladds on Bexleyheath who managed an extensive acreage of glasshouses. The Miles at Normandy Farm along with Myrtle and Venners Farm in the Northumberland Heath/North End area cultivated large areas of orchards.

The Perry Street junction on the Sidcup By-Pass. This was a twice daily traffic calming measure when the farmer of Frogpool Farm on Perry Street transferred his herd of Jersey Cattle to and from their grazing area on the north side of the road. this picture shows them returning home. Such a manoeuvre may have been expected shortly after the road was built (1926), this, extraordinarily, was taking place in 1961!

Village Life

At the beginning of the nineteenth century most of the population of what we now know as Bexley London Borough was concentrated in a number of villages; Bexley, Crayford and Erith being the largest. But even in these, buildings were largely concentrated along one street. The villages were ancient; Bexley, Footscray, Crayford, Erith, North Cray and East Wickham all date from Saxon times. They were strategically placed; Footscray, where the London to Maidstone Road crossed the River Cray: Bexley, where the Dartford to Eltham and the Orpington to Crayford Roads crossed the River Cray; Crayford, where the important London to Dover Road could ford the Cray and Erith at a haven on the River Thames.

In the village rich and poor lived side-by-side with substantial and fashionable houses alongside small cottages. Central to village life was the parish church though by the middle of the nineteenth century, non-conformist churches of various denominations were also a feature of the villages. Inns and beer houses were a vital part

Footscray village, from an early nineteenth-century aquatint. The "Seven Stars" can be seen on the extreme right. All the other buildings are now gone.

Village Life

The village of Crayford from Crayford Bridge, 1832. The High Street was widened in 1937. The whole of the eastern side was demolished. A number of buildings on the western side survive, however.

of the village. In the 1850s Bexley village could boast half-a-dozen public houses and as many beer houses. Shopkeepers and traders included a hairdresser, two tailors, a plumber and painter, two carpenters, two grocers, a smith, two butchers, a baker, a draper and a boot and shoemaker; in fact a much wider range than Bexley village offers today.

Villages were also industrial centres. There were flour mills at Footscray, Bexley and Erith; tanneries at Bexley and Crayford; barge-builders at Erith and coach builders at Bexley and Footscray. Crayford was the most industrialised village with several extensive silk and calico printing works.

By the mid-nineteenth century each village had its own school mostly under the auspices of the Church of England's National Society for the Promotion of the Education of the Poor. Some of these schools such as Foster's School at East Wickham and Footscray National School are still being used as schools (though the latter is now a private school); others survive but serve other purposes such as Bexley National School (now offices) and North Cray National School (now a private residence).

Outside of the village the rest of the population lived in scattered farms and hamlets such as Blackfen, Upton and Picardy.

These often housed employees of the many large country houses in the district such as the hamlet of Blendon serving Blendon Hall.

The old villages have now been swallowed up by suburbia and redeveloped or, in the case of North Cray, virtually wiped out for road widening. Yet in many ways they survive as a focal point for local communities.

Erith in 1750, from a print by John Boydell. At this date the village of Erith was little more than a single street, running parallel to and, as this illustration vividly shows, owing its existence to the River Thames.

Village Life

Bexley village, from a watercolour by I T Wilson, c.1865-70, looking east from near the junction of the High Street and Bourne Road. In the centre is the "Miller's Arms", rebuilt in 1899. "The George" was rebuilt in 1878. The building on the extreme left survives as C C Flint and Co, 79, High Street, Bexley.

Victorian Sidcup

Hatherley Road, Sidcup, c.1904. This road was among the first of the new roads to be laid out in Sidcup. The houses shown date from the 1870s and are a mixture of semi-detached and detached houses, highly ornamented. In the last twenty years the character of the road has changed dramatically as re-development has taken place, but a number of these fine houses survive.

While there had been a settlement at Sidcup as early as 1254 the poor quality of the soil ensured that there was not great growth and still by the beginning of the nineteenth century it was no more than a hamlet. The nucleus of Sidcup was really nothing more than an inn and a smithy and a few cottages and houses scattered loosely near the top of the present day Sidcup Hill which formed part of the London to Maidstone Road.

To the north lay the equally as old and rather larger hamlet of Halfway Street. In the 1840s both these communities had chapels-of-ease built but there had been no significant growth. Plans for a railway line to Sidcup and along the path of the present "Dartford Loop" line had been bandied about since 1837 and 1844.

High Street, Sidcup, c.1905. In the space of forty years this stretch of the London to Maidstone Road had been transformed from passing through open countryside to the bustling shopping thoroughfare seen here.

Victorian Sidcup

Members of the Tolhurst family in the grounds of the Grange. This house was situated near the junction of Cross Road and Rectory Lane. The house was demolished to make way for Old Forge Way in the mid 1930s.

The line was opened by the South Eastern Railway on 1st September 1866. The station was named 'Sidcup' though was situated closer to Halfway Street than Sidcup itself. From the outset a commuter-geared service was provided to London Bridge, Cannon Street and Charing Cross and the owners of a tract of land between the station and the further side of Main Road were able to dispose of their indifferent mixture of clays and gravels as building plots. The start of development was slow, mainly because main drainage did not reach Sidcup until 1883. Gradually houses were built and were taken, mainly by City merchants, brokers and

professionals moving from the older areas of Clapham, Balham and Streatham, etc.
One of the earliest roads to be developed was Hatherley Road in 1872 with substantial villas. It was paralleled by smaller villas and cottages in Birkbeck Road for tradesmen, artisans and labourers.

The Drive, c.1905, looking north from near the junction with Rectory Lane. The Drive was developed slowly and at this date a number of plots remained undeveloped. On the left hand side in the foreground is a field, part of Manor Farm. The young trees have now reached maturity.

Victorian Sidcup

AT NOMINAL RESERVES.

SIDCUP, KENT,

Five minutes from Sidcup and ten minutes from Pope Street Stations of Great Eastern Railway.

Particulars, Plan, and Conditions of Sale

OF

83 PLOTS

OF VALUABLE

Freehold Building Land,

BEING THE SECOND PORTION OF THE

"LONGLANDS PARK ESTATE,"

HAVING EXCELLENT FRONTAGES TO THE

Park Hill and other well - made Roads.

Water and Gas Mains are laid on the Estate;

ALSO

TWO WELL-BUILT DETACHED VILLA RESIDENCES

KNOWN AS

"Hurst Cottage" and "Loxley House,"

Each containing Three Reception Rooms, Six Bed Rooms, Bath Room, and Domestic Offices; both let at £70 and £75 per Annum each;

Which will be Sold by Auction, by Messrs.

BAKER AND SONS

AT THE "BLACK HORSE HOTEL," SIDCUP,

On MONDAY, AUGUST 18th, 1890,

AT TWO FOR HALF-PAST PRECISELY.

Possession will be given to any of the Lots 97 to 179, both inclusive, on payment of £10 per cent. deposit, the balance of Purchase-money being payable by ten half-yearly instalments, if desired.

FREE CONVEYANCES.

A limited number of FREE RETURN RAILWAY TICKETS will be issued to London Buyers by the Train leaving Charing Cross at 12.45, Cannon Street at 12.55, and London Bridge at 12.59. Luncheon will be provided at the place of Sale, at 1.30 o'clock, immediately on the arrival of the 12.45 Train from London.

Particulars, Plan, and Conditions of Sale may be had at the place of Sale; of

Messrs. BANNISTER, WILLIAMS & RAM, Solicitors, 13, John Street, Bedford Row, W.C.; of
Mr. R. TOMLINSON, Architect to the Estate, 12, John Street, Bedford Row, W.C., and Gunnersbury Station, London, W.; and of
Messrs. BAKER & SONS, Land Agents and Surveyors, 11, Queen Victoria Street, London, E.C.

Development took place generally on a field-by-field basis. Among the principal developers were George Hawkins, who built many houses at Longlands and central Sidcup, and Thomas Knight, who built houses around Sidcup Hill.

From the late 1870s social matters grew in importance - after all Sidcup was a New Town comparable with Hemel Hempstead or Stevenage today: religious groups, local societies and clubs abounded, and public buildings including an Infants' School, a Fire Station and a Public Hall were constructed.

To cope with the day-to-day needs of this middle/high class society, shops were developed along most of the High Street. These catered for a 'quality' trade and Sidcup was, in fact, quite a shopping Mecca for occupants of large houses from a distance around.

Sale particulars of a section of the Longlands Park Estate to be sold by auction at the "Black Horse Hotel", 1890.

Victorian Erith

The most striking aspect of Victorian Erith and the immediate surroundings for which it was the focus was the sheer variety of its historical experience. The general trends of the town's history fit uncomfortably into this book's title. The town was in part a middle class suburb, in part a major shopping centre, in part heavily industrialised with associated areas of working class housing and in part a riverside town and in part a leisure resort.

In the early years of the nineteenth century its population was less than 2,000 and the town was centred tightly around the High Street. The parish church of St John stood a half-mile distant from the town centre along West Street. The town was flanked by larger houses such as the Manor

Erith High Street looking south east, a view of c.1900. The causeway and its fence provided a suitable view and support for those described so waspishly by George Sala in the 1850s (see p. 20).

Victorian Erith

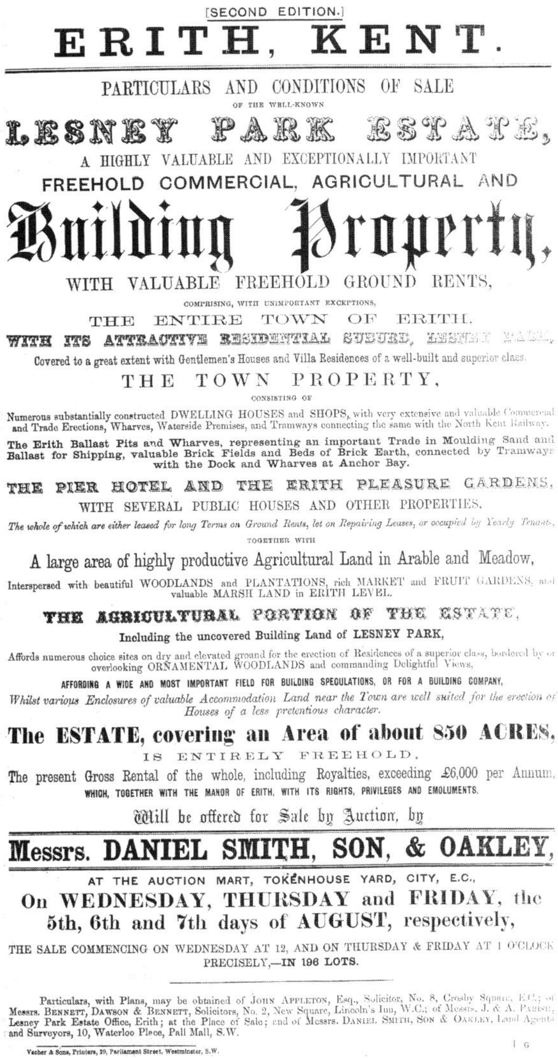

[SECOND EDITION.]

ERITH, KENT.

PARTICULARS AND CONDITIONS OF SALE

OF THE WELL-KNOWN

LESNEY PARK ESTATE,

A HIGHLY VALUABLE AND EXCEPTIONALLY IMPORTANT

FREEHOLD COMMERCIAL, AGRICULTURAL AND

Building Property,

WITH VALUABLE FREEHOLD GROUND RENTS,

COMPRISING, WITH UNIMPORTANT EXCEPTIONS,

THE ENTIRE TOWN OF ERITH.

WITH ITS ATTRACTIVE RESIDENTIAL SUBURB, LESNEY PARK,

Covered to a great extent with Gentlemen's Houses and Villa Residences of a well-built and superior class.

THE TOWN PROPERTY,

CONSISTING OF

Numerous substantially constructed DWELLING HOUSES and SHOPS, with very extensive and valuable Commercial and Trade Erections, Wharves, Waterside Premises, and Tramways connecting the same with the North Kent Railway.

The Erith Ballast Pits and Wharves, representing an important Trade in Moulding Sand and Ballast for Shipping, valuable Brick Fields and Beds of Brick Earth, connected by Tramways with the Dock and Wharves at Anchor Bay.

THE PIER HOTEL AND THE ERITH PLEASURE GARDENS,

WITH SEVERAL PUBLIC HOUSES AND OTHER PROPERTIES,

The whole of which are either leased for long Terms on Ground Rents, let on Repairing Leases, or occupied by Yearly Tenants,

TOGETHER WITH

A large area of highly productive Agricultural Land in Arable and Meadow,

Interspersed with beautiful WOODLANDS and PLANTATIONS, rich MARKET and FRUIT GARDENS, and valuable MARSH LAND in ERITH LEVEL.

THE AGRICULTURAL PORTION OF THE ESTATE,

Including the uncovered Building Land of LESNEY PARK,

Affords numerous choice sites on dry and elevated ground for the erection of Residences of a superior class, bordered by or overlooking ORNAMENTAL WOODLANDS and commanding Delightful Views,

AFFORDING A WIDE AND MOST IMPORTANT FIELD FOR BUILDING SPECULATIONS, OR FOR A BUILDING COMPANY,

Whilst various Enclosures of valuable Accommodation Land near the Town are well suited for the erection of Houses of a less pretentious character.

The ESTATE, covering an Area of about 850 ACRES,

IS ENTIRELY FREEHOLD,

The present Gross Rental of the whole, including Royalties, exceeding £6,000 per Annum,

WHICH, TOGETHER WITH THE MANOR OF ERITH, WITH ITS RIGHTS, PRIVILEGES AND EMOLUMENTS,

Will be offered for Sale by Auction, by

Messrs. DANIEL SMITH, SON, & OAKLEY,

AT THE AUCTION MART, TOKENHOUSE YARD, CITY, E.C.,

On WEDNESDAY, THURSDAY and FRIDAY, the 5th, 6th and 7th days of AUGUST, respectively,

THE SALE COMMENCING ON WEDNESDAY AT 12, AND ON THURSDAY & FRIDAY AT 1 O'CLOCK PRECISELY,—IN 196 LOTS.

Particulars, with Plans, may be obtained of JOHN APPLETON, Esq., Solicitor, No. 8, Crosby Square, E.C.; of Messrs. BENNETT, DAWSON & BENNETT, Solicitors, No. 2, New Square, Lincoln's Inn, W.C.; of Messrs. J. & A. PARISH, Lesney Park Estate Office, Erith; at the Place of Sale; and of Messrs. DANIEL SMITH, SON & OAKLEY, Land Agents and Surveyors, 10, Waterloo Place, Pall Mall, S.W.

Vacher & Sons, Printers, 29, Parliament Street, Westminster, S.W. 1 G

The title page of the auction catalogue for the Lesney Park Estate in 1874. This was essentially the whole town of Erith owned until then by Wheatley Family.

House occupied by the Wheatley Family, which stood at the end of a large avenue of elm trees and to the east the grander and more distant Belvedere House occupied by the Eardley family. The town earned its living from a mixture of agriculture and river-related activity. Its sheltered position and gravel foreshore made it one of the few suitable riverside landing places between Woolwich and Gravesend. It housed a small fishing fleet and associated services.

Briefly in the Tudor period there was a small Royal Naval Dockyard. The only industry in the town in the early nineteenth century was gravel, sand and loam quarrying from the area around the present Fraser Road. The nineteenth century journalist, George Sala, writing in 1852 was little impressed by the energy of the town's inhabitants. He commented "three-fourths of the male population and the whole of the female and infant ditto are always loitering in doorways or sprawling amicably in that part of the road where there should be a gutter".

Erith's expansion rose to a climax as the century progressed; in 1881 its population was 9,500 and in 1901, 25,000. This growth was almost totally caused by the town's developing industry. Even by 1900 only a small minority of the population were London-bound suburban commuters. The major catalyst in this development was the coming of the railway in 1849. Pre-dating this or housing and industrial development was the town's failed attempt to become a riverside pleasure resort. In 1842 the Wheatley estate built a pier to the east of the town and a hotel immediately onshore. The land to the east was laid out as a garden with an arboretum much in the style of Gravesend's Rosherville Gardens. Residential development commenced in the 1850s with the first fragmentation of the Wheatley estate to the south of Bexley Road. In 1858 the Manor House was pulled down and in 1874 the whole estate - the vast majority of the town - auctioned. Housing development continued in piecemeal fashion as the century progressed with rows of terraced housing nearby to the industry to the town's west and east and more substantial middle class housing on the outskirts.

The town's industry was in three distinct locations. The first area to be developed was to the riverside to the east. Here near Anchor Bay, Easton and Anderson established the Thames Ironworks in 1864. Brickmaking was also carried out nearby and bricks were transported from Anchor Bay Wharf. At the 1874 auction the Beadle family bought the pleasure gardens and converted it into a coal wharf. On the riverfront to the west of the town the Callender Bitumen, Telegraph and Waterproof Company was founded in 1880. As the need for cable grew, the firm increasingly specialised becoming the Callender

The pier and hotel built for the Erith resort. By the 1890s, when this photograph was taken, the gardens had become a coal depot and further downstream a shipbuilding yard. Beadles, who managed the coal depot retained the hotel as their offices.

Victorian Erith

Pier Road looking east from near the corner with Queen's Road. This was the business and professional area, as along with the bank the road also housed solicitors' offices, a doctor's surgery and the local newspaper. The tram lines date the picture to some time after 1905.

Cable Construction Company in 1896. Closer to the town centre near Parish's pit the Nordenfeldt Gun Company, later amalgamated with Vickers, opened a munitions works in 1887. Nearby the American based firm of Fraser and Chalmers, makers of mining machinery, opened a works in 1891.

The eastern end of The Avenue, Erith c.1900. This impressive elm lined road led from the railway to the site of the Manor House. Lesney Farm occupied the site in the early twentieth century.

A view of the early 1880s along West Street from the church spire to the town. The view shows the isolated position of St John's Church, left so after the 'migration' of the town centre south-eastwards. It also shows the ample amount of green space still remaining. The Gas Works opened in 1862.

Victorian Northumberland Heath

In 1800 Northumberland Heath was a 200 acre area of heathland similar in character to Dartford Heath today. It was common land under the control of Erith parish but became part of the Wheatley Estate under the Erith Enclosure Act of 1815. For much of the nineteenth century the principal buildings were the parish workhouse or "spike" and a mill.
Residential development started in the 1880s and by 1900 a thriving community had established itself with a parish church of St Paul and a school on Brook Street. The very early years of the twentieth century were a busy period for the area as it was the tram terminus for both Erith and Bexley's trams and, for a few years until through working started, all passengers were required to change cars.

Bexley Road, Northumberland Heath in about 1912. Limewood Road is the turning near the end of the parade of shops. Lorne Mash's dairy shop indicates the rural nature of the surrounding area.

Victorian Northumberland Heath

A view (above) of about 1907 towards Erith. Colyers Lane is just beyond the large tree on the right, part of a large orchard. Brook Street turns to the left just by the Duke of Northumberland pub.

Looking north along Brook Street from the junction with Mill Road. The terrace on the right, though seemingly uniform was built in stages after 1895. Brook Street School also of 1895 stands opposite.

Victorian Belvedere

Belvedere, although connected administratively and economically with Erith, had its own identity and character. Its development as housing was predated by the tiny hamlet of Picardy and the large Belvedere House occupied by the Eardley family. Development of the area grew from the enclosure and sub-division of Lessness Heath by the Eardleys and others. This process started in the mid-nineteenth century with the laying out of the area around Belvedere Park and was greatly

Halt Robin Road, Belvedere, in the early years of this century. The view is looking east from near the junction with Bunker's Hill towards the junction with Park Road. The large semi-detached houses on the left date from the 1850s.

Station Road in Lower Belvedere. This area of small terraced streets had only just started its development at the end of the nineteenth century. The road that the tram lines follow to St Augustine's Church was not built until after 1870. The trams came in 1905.

accelerated by the opening of Belvedere Station in 1859. The West Heath area was developed after 1882. The substantial homes of Upper Belvedere were complemented by the building (1853) and consecration (1861) of All Saints Church. While Upper Belvedere cultivated its rural village atmosphere, Lower Belvedere provided working class housing for riverside factory employees.

Victorian Belvedere

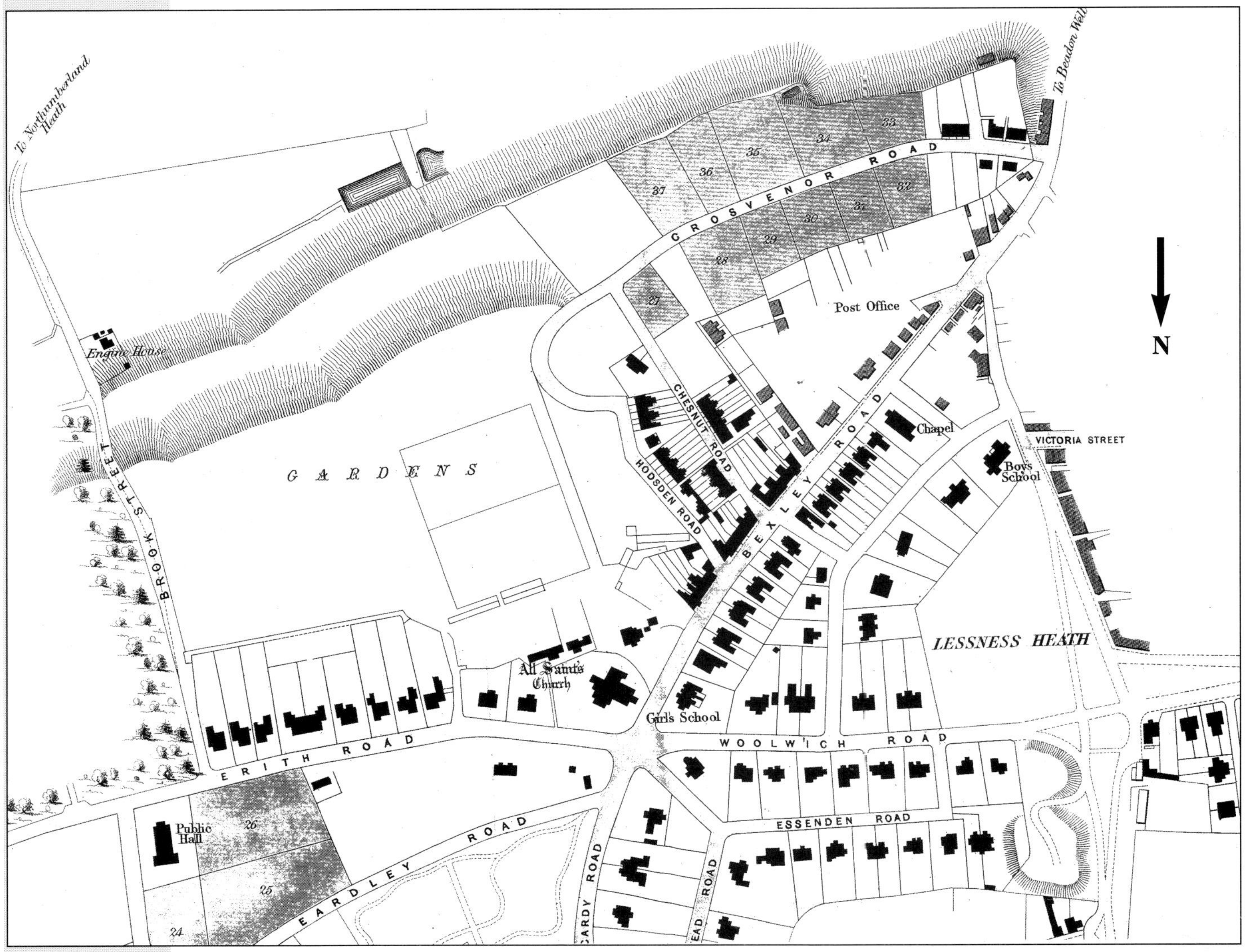

Part of a plan from sales particulars for the Belvedere Estate, 1876.

Victorian Bexley

At the beginning of the nineteenth century Bexley Village was much as it had been in medieval times, a mixture of houses, cottages, shops and pubs, along both sides of a winding High Street. In the latter half of the eighteenth century several Georgian houses were built including High Street House and Cray House, as well as Styleman's Almshouses, which brought a new elegance to the village without expanding its size.

Clapgate Cottages, Bexley High Street, c.1890. These charming old weather-boarded cottages were demolished to make way for the Freemantle Hall *(see p. 36)*.

Victorian Bexley

Marl House, Parkhill Road, Bexley, c.1886 and (opposite page) c.1910. The old weather-boarded Marl House with its wooden fence gave way to its extraordinary looking replacement in 1891. The new house was for Hargreaves Rogers, Sheriff of the City of London and a leading player in Bexley affairs. Marl House was demolished in 1962 to make way for a housing development (see p. 91). The Victorian pillar box survives, however.

In the first half of the nineteenth century some modest developments took place in the form of cottages in Bourne Road north of the National School which had been built in 1834, and in the northern part of what is now Albert Road. This latter development included a new pub, the "Black Horse".

In 1866 the Dartford Loop Line opened with a station at Bexley very close to the High Street, and the line itself bi-secting the High Street by means of a bridge. Today as we pass under it we are scarcely aware of its existence but in 1866 the impact on the quiet village must have been phenomenal. It was not long before housing development followed. The largest estate development was the Parkhurst-Knoll Road estate on the western edge of the village. A sales catalogue for part of this estate makes it quite clear that this development was intended for the

Victorian Bexley

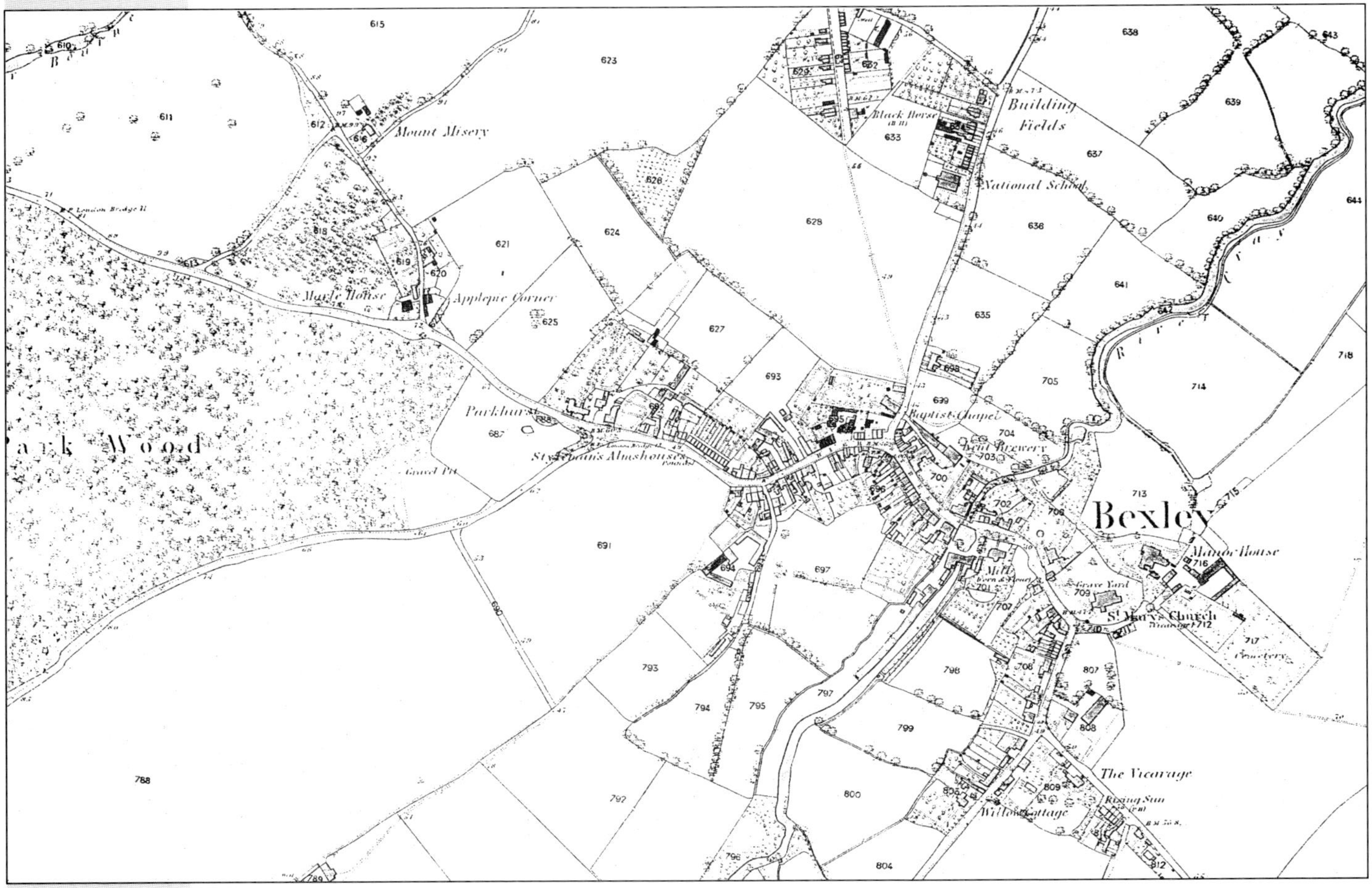

Ordnance Survey maps of Bexley village, 1862 and 1895, illustrating the development that followed the arrival of the railway.

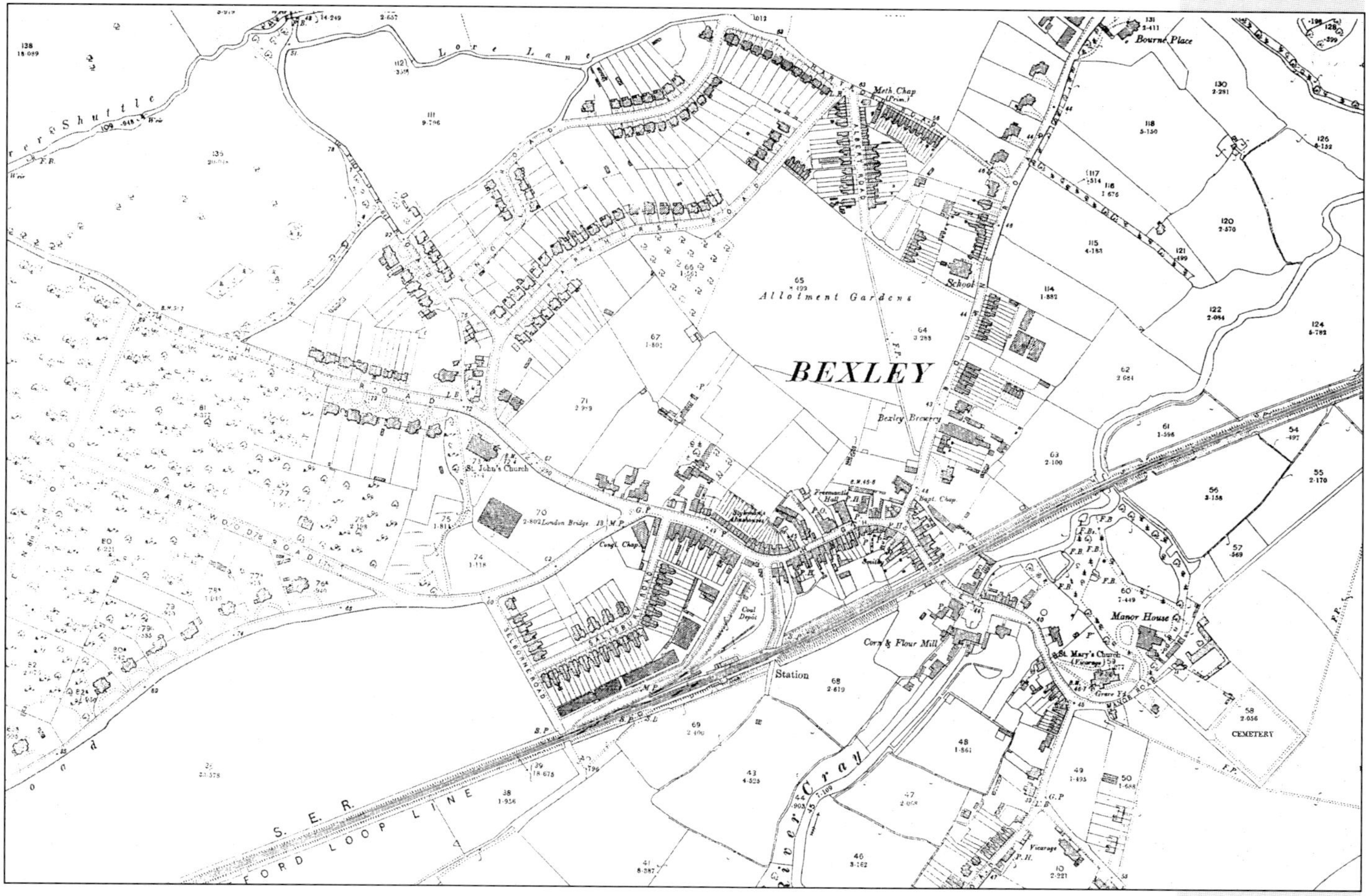
Lore Lane
Bourne Place
Meth. Chap. (Prim.)
School
Allotment Gardens
BEXLEY
Bexley Brewery
St. John's Church
London Bridge 13 M.P.
Cong'l. Chap.
Bapt. Chap.
Smithy
Coal Depot
Station
Corn & Flour Mill
Manor House
St. Mary's Church
Grave Yd.
CEMETERY
Vicarage
River Cray
S. E. R.
LOOP LINE

Victorian Bexley

The new 'suburb' of Bexley; the Parkhurst Estate c.1890 seen from the spire of St John's Church. The spire of the chapel-of-ease at Oaklands Road, Bexleyheath is visible in the distance.

city commuter. The estate fitted the configuration of the field over which it was built. It was truly suburban in style with effective use of bends in the new roads, a feature of suburbia.

This middle-class development built c.1878 - 1881, was made up of detached and semi-detached two-storey houses built in grey brick, with bay windows, some with highly ornate decorative features, unlike anything Bexley Village had seen before. Other developments included the Salisbury Road Estate, next to the station in a field cut off by the railway line. This consisted mainly of small leasehold semi-detached houses. Other developments included large detached villas along the North Cray Road and a development of very large houses above the village at Coldblow. The prime development occurred out along Hurst Road in the form of a number of fine houses set in their own grounds backing on to Bexley Park Wood and fronted by a fine commanding view across the village to the North Downs. These were the homes of wealthy businessmen and professional men working in the City, who included the Chairman of the Chatham and South Eastern Railway Company which had built the Dartford Loop Line.

High Street, Bexley, 1912. The new upper-middle classes of the Parkhurst Estate required smarter shopping facilities than had previously been on offer in the village. This view shows Victorian shops on either side of the street. Oxford Terrace in the centre would not look out of place in Blackheath. It dates from 1878. In the distance the spire of the church of St John the Evangelist can be seen; it was added to the church in 1890, some eight years after the body of the church had been completed.

Victorian Bexley

The arrival of this new middle class no doubt created a tension with the old-established village families. Certainly the face of the village changed considerably before the end of the century. Pubs such as the "Miller's Arms" and the "Rising Sun" were rebuilt, new Victorian parades of shops were built, a new community facility, The Freemantle Hall, replaced old cottages; a new Anglican church as well as Baptist and Congregational Chapels was founded. The present Bexley Village Conservation Area is essentially Victorian.

The Freemantle Hall c.1905. It was built in 1894 by public subscription and other efforts on a site, previously occupied by Clapgate Cottages (see p. 29), given by William Freemantle in 1891. The clock was not installed until 1920.

Victorian Bexleyheath

At the opening of the nineteenth century Bexleyheath was a tract of rough open common land, unpopulated and uncultivated, the only buildings of note being the "Golden Lion", a coaching inn dating from about 1730 at the western end of the Heath and a windmill in what is now Mayplace Road East. Yet by the end of the century, it had become a populous town with, including part of Welling, over 8,000 inhabitants.

Across the Heath ran the London to Dover Road and in the late eighteenth century it was a notorious haunt of highwaymen. Though the Heath appears from official records to have been

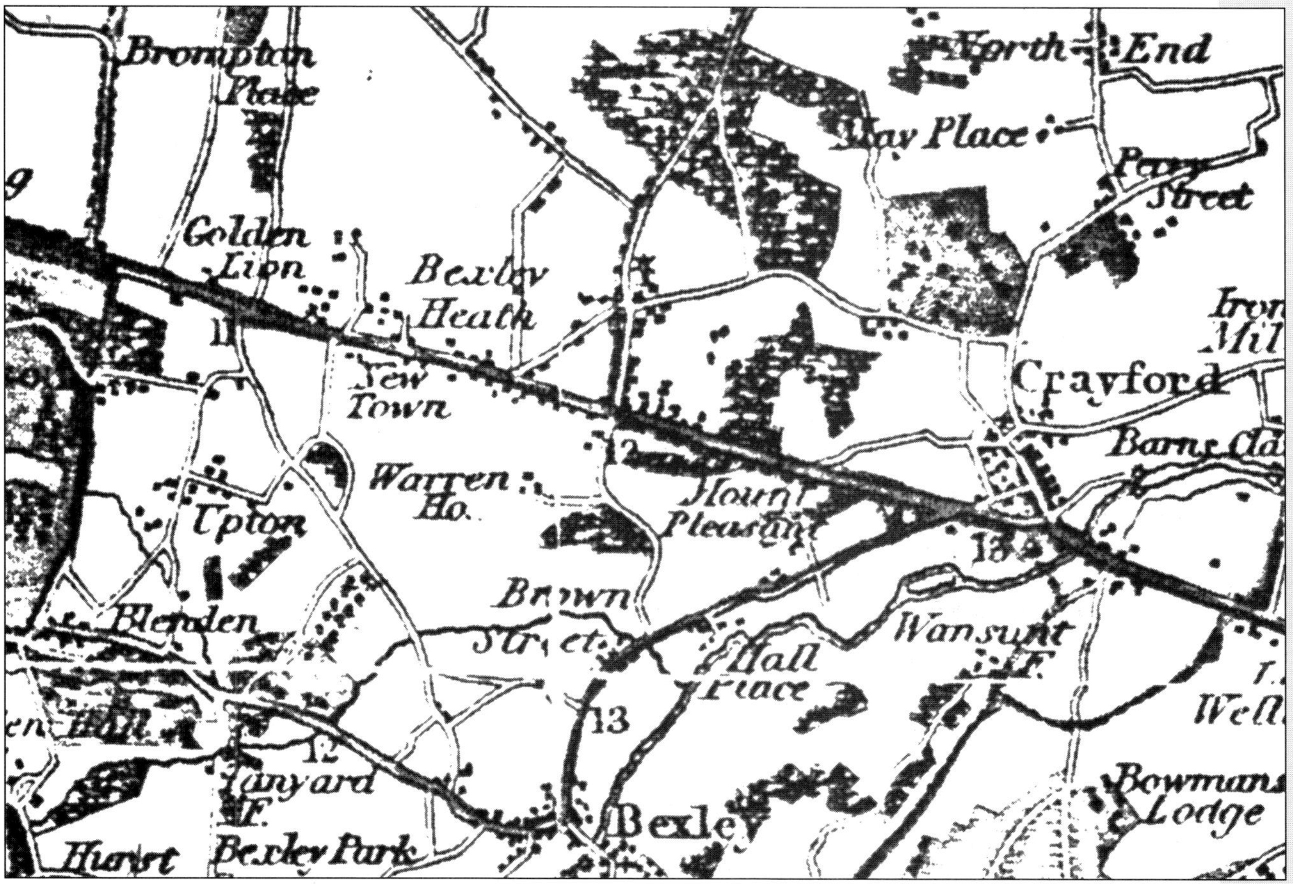

Part of Greenwood's map of Kent, 1821, showing the "New Town" at Bexley Heath.

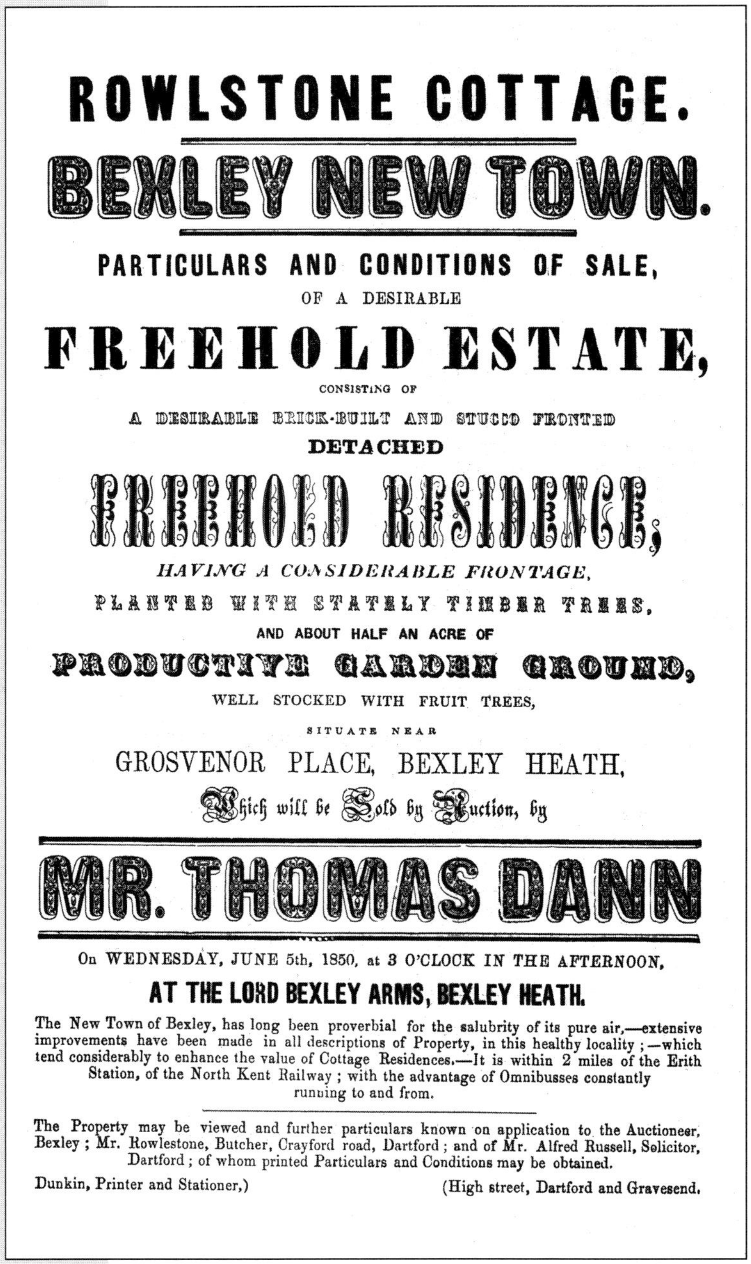
ROWLSTONE COTTAGE.

BEXLEY NEW TOWN.

PARTICULARS AND CONDITIONS OF SALE,
OF A DESIRABLE

FREEHOLD ESTATE,
CONSISTING OF
A DESIRABLE BRICK-BUILT AND STUCCO FRONTED
DETACHED

FREEHOLD RESIDENCE,
HAVING A CONSIDERABLE FRONTAGE,
PLANTED WITH STATELY TIMBER TREES,
AND ABOUT HALF AN ACRE OF
PRODUCTIVE GARDEN GROUND,
WELL STOCKED WITH FRUIT TREES,
SITUATE NEAR
GROSVENOR PLACE, BEXLEY HEATH,
Which will be Sold by Auction, by

MR. THOMAS DANN

On WEDNESDAY, JUNE 5th, 1850, at 3 O'CLOCK IN THE AFTERNOON,
AT THE LORD BEXLEY ARMS, BEXLEY HEATH.

The New Town of Bexley, has long been proverbial for the salubrity of its pure air,—extensive improvements have been made in all descriptions of Property, in this healthy locality;—which tend considerably to enhance the value of Cottage Residences.—It is within 2 miles of the Erith Station, of the North Kent Railway; with the advantage of Omnibusses constantly running to and from.

The Property may be viewed and further particulars known on application to the Auctioneer, Bexley; Mr. Rowlestone, Butcher, Crayford road, Dartford; and of Mr. Alfred Russell, Solicitor, Dartford; of whom printed Particulars and Conditions may be obtained.

Dunkin, Printer and Stationer,) (High street, Dartford and Gravesend.

unpopulated, there is evidence to suggest that from the 1770s squatters or "sojourners" were living there probably employed in the expanding textile industry at Crayford. In the early nineteenth century local landowners moved to prevent squatters acquiring rights of possession by getting an Act of Parliament to authorise the enclosure of the Heath and its partition among the freeholders. As the Heath lay partly in Bexley parish and partly in Crayford, two Acts were required. The Crayford one was passed in 1812 and the Bexley one in 1814. The Enclosure Commissioner's awards were published in 1819 and 1820. Allotments of various sizes were awarded to no fewer than 107 recipients in the Bexley part.

In 1816 it is recorded that there were 12 cottages on the Heath; by 1822, there were 18 cottages and 100 houses. Fifteen years later there were the same number of houses, but no fewer than 170 cottages. The district was at this time known as Bexley New Town or Bexley Heath New Town. The community was centred on the Market Place and along the Main Road and was a strange mixture of substantial mansions such as Oak House and West Lodge and mean cottages. As with new towns today, public opinion on its merits were varied. William Cobbett in 1821 used the terms "ugly" and "shabby" in his description of it whereas Pigot's directory for 1832 stated that "a

Sale particulars of Rowlstone Cottage, 1850; even at this date "Bexley New Town" was still being used to describe the now well-established settlement.

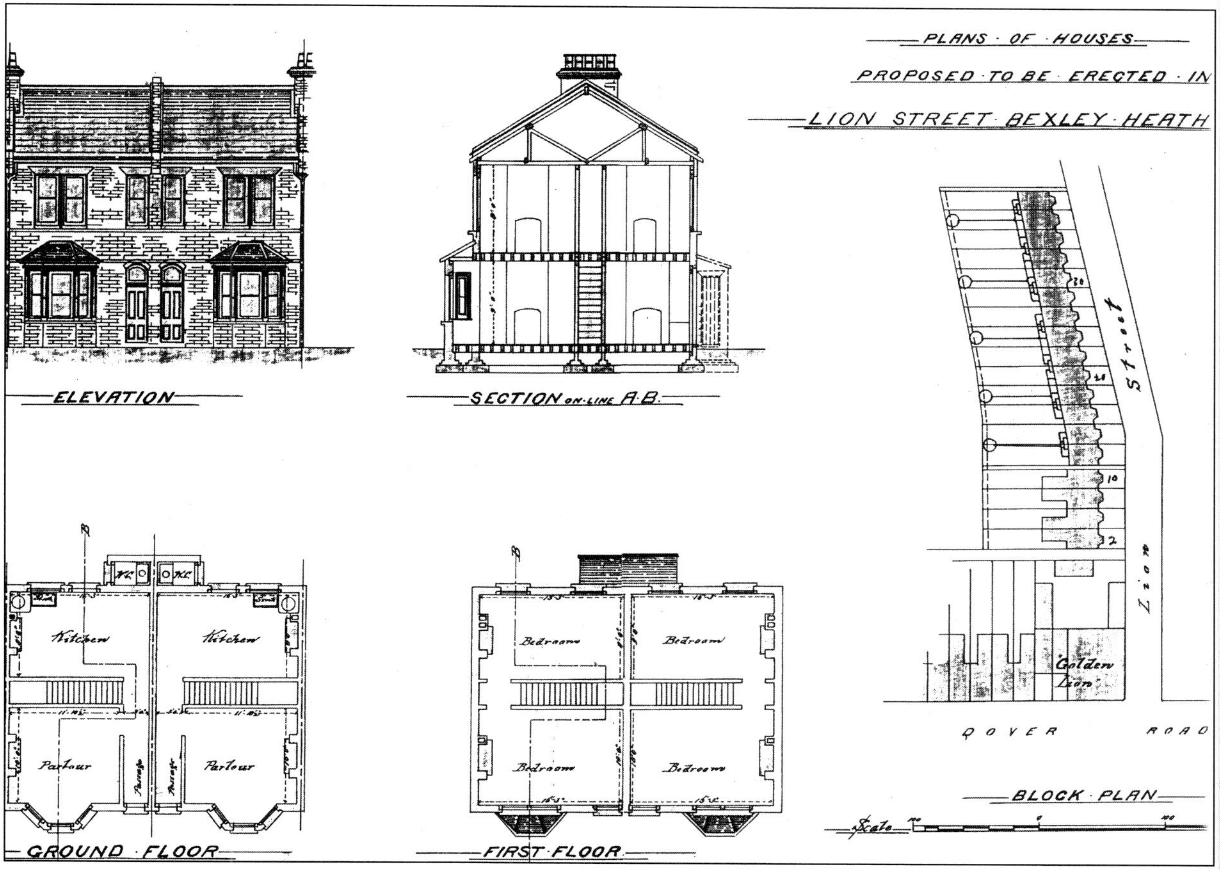

Plans of terraced housing in Lion Street (now West Street), Bexleyheath, 1885. The houses are "two-up-two-down" with outside toilets.

great number of good houses have recently been erected here; and the situation is considered as one of the most healthy, as it is one of the most pleasing in this part of the country".

In the mid-nineteenth century the majority of the population were either employed as agricultural labourers, in the textile industry at Crayford or in domestic service. It has been estimated that of its population of about 2,000 in 1851, two thirds of the working population came from further afield than Bexley or Crayford.

With the growth of housing an infrastructure for the new community gradually developed: churches of many denominations, shops, public

Victorian Bexleyheath

Oak House School, c.1900. Some of the earliest buildings on the Heath were substantial villas such as this, which was built in about 1817, fronting on to the Broadway. It became a school in 1863, and from 1903 was used as council offices. It was demolished in 1976.

Christ Church under construction, c.1875, from the north. Buildings in the Broadway can be seen through the church. Building began in 1872 but it was hindered by lack of funds. The planned tower and spire were never built.

houses, schools, public halls, and the town's own newspaper, "The Bexleyheath Observer". By the end of the century Bexleyheath (as it was by then officially known) was an established town. Most of the development had taken place close to the main road or in streets running directly off it. Most of the building consisted of lower-middle and working class streets of bay-fronted terraced houses, typical of much of the outer-London

Hides, c.1875. In 1851, Henry and George Hide purchased the business of Collier's Emporium at 85 The Broadway. By the 1930s it had developed into a modern department store. It was demolished to make way for the present Broadway Shopping Centre.

Victorian Bexleyheath

A Victorian parade of shops on the north side of the Broadway, between Abbey Road and Harcourt Road. As the Broadway developed commercially, houses were converted into shops and purpose-built shops such as these were built.

suburbs developing at this time. The two largest of such estates were the Oaklands estate developed by Alers Hankey south of the Broadway near Upton and the Sandford estate on the north side.

The opening of the Bexleyheath Railway in 1895 did not immediately lead to further housing development; indeed it further stimulated market gardening for which the district was noted. There were very many nurseries in Bexleyheath and the Victorian town was surrounded by farms, fields and orchards.

Bexleyheath Market Place; the opening of the Clock Tower in 1912. Bexleyheath had by this date matured into a bustling town with a population of over 9,000.

Victorian Bexleyheath

Upland School nearing completion, 1895. The provision of schooling for the rapidly growing population of the new town was a major problem. Until 1894 it had remained under the exclusive control of the church authorities. The Bexley School Board, whose initials adorn this school, was created in that year.

Victorian Bexleyheath

Looking north from the roof of Christ Church, c.1900, showing the gradual spread northwards of Bexleyheath. New facilities for the town can be seen in the shape of Bexleyheath Cemetery, opened in 1879 at a cost of £2,700 and the Board School (in the centre of the picture) in Upland Road opened in 1895. However, countryside remains very much in evidence and Burr Farm, to the right of the school, did not disappear until the 1930s.

Victorian Bexleyheath

Looking west from the roof of the Congregational Church, c.1900. The Broadway was the focus for the earliest development on the Heath, plots fronting it had cottages and shops built on them. This photograph graphically demonstrates how the narrow plots at the rear of the buildings were gradually given over to stores, stables and workshops as the Broadway was commercialised. On the horizon in the centre can be seen the steeple of the old chapel-of-ease in Oaklands Road, the body of which was demolished in 1878. It was replaced by Christ Church which can be seen to the right. Its steeple was never built.

Crayford Garden Suburb

Crayford's population in 1911 was just over 6,000. In 1916 it had trebled to around 18,000. This phenomenal increase was caused by the re-opening and expansion of the Vickers armaments factory in response to the Army's insatiable needs during the First World War.

An aerial view looking north of the Vickers works and the west end of the Garden Suburb in 1929. It amply demonstrates the scale of the company's operation and the proximity of home and work. The Princesses Theatre is the prominent white building on the far left. It was demolished in 1957. The open square crossed by the rail line in the left foreground was the centre piece of the factory.

Crayford Garden Suburb

Green Walk very shortly after completion of the estate in 1916. Note the varied roof lines, the gentle curve of the road, spartan gardens and narrowness of the street.

Before 1912 Crayford had been in a steady decline. The end of the Boer War curtailed Vickers' production of the machine gun and the company diversified into motor car manufacture. This ceased in 1910 causing great hardship to the town. Its fortunes revived with the start of World War One and the consequent need for guns and ammunition, a need made more acute by the inability of Government factories to meet demand. Vickers were the sole producer of the machine gun as developed by Hiram Maxim and demand rose as the war progressed. In early 1916 production was at 40 per month and two years later stood at 1,200 a month.

The factory and its workforce expanded. At its peak the firm employed 14,500 and Crayford, along with other munition towns, Erith, Dartford and Woolwich, enjoyed unprecedented prosperity. As in these other towns the expansion created a considerable housing problem. Solutions were sought around Woolwich by the construction of temporary hutments at Eltham and East

Green Walk in 1938. Blossom, happy children and attentive parents, a demonstration of the social harmony that Garden Suburb designers hoped their schemes would generate. An aspiration founded in no small part by William Morris, designer, writer, socialist, romantic and Bexleyheath resident.

Crayford Garden Suburb

The Princesses Theatre on Crayford Waterside in about 1920. The theatre was opened in 1916 and was built by Vickers to provide entertainment for their staff. It was an early location for watching silent movies which were accompanied by the theatre organ or orchestra. Seats cost between 1s. 10d. and 2s. 4d. It later became the Ritz Cinema but was demolished in 1957.

Wickham and later by the Well Hall (Progress) Estate. Vickers' answer in Crayford was the building of the Garden Suburb or Barnes Cray Estate to the north east of the town. Between 1915 and 1916 six hundred cottages were built. The firm also provided its staff (and therefore the town) with other amenities. The present Town Hall was built as a staff canteen and the Princesses Theatre was built on the riverside. The company was able to draw on their experience of a similar project at Vickerstown adjacent to their works at Barrow, Cumbria.

A cartoon from a volume entitled The Crayford Sketch Book 1918 produced by Vickers' Drawing Office. The decrepit snail driven tram is a far more eloquent description of pre-war Crayford than a volume of statistics.

The housing estate was their most enduring contribution. It was designed by Gordon Allen, an architect specialising in vernacular styled housing developments of small, inexpensively built units using modern materials.

The houses were designed in a variety of styles each containing at least three bedrooms, a sunny living room and hot and cold water. More than half were built from (rendered) concrete walls; the remainder were cavity brick thus utilising a

Crayford Garden Suburb

variety of materials at a period of wartime. The scheme was supervised by the Housing Organisation Society which attempted to keep costs low. The building costs of many of the houses was merely £200 and the total cost including utilities averaged £325.

The scheme was parallel in conception and design with Eltham's Well Hall Estate. The latter was built on a deliberately intricate street plan in a wide variety of forms utilising an equally wide range of materials and decorative features. These Crayford aspired to but did not quite equal. The estate did however avoid the worst excesses of a grid plan with uniform terraces; it even included planned areas of open space and, along with the other social amenities, Vickers provided their workers with housing and social facilities far in advance of those enjoyed by industrial workers elsewhere.

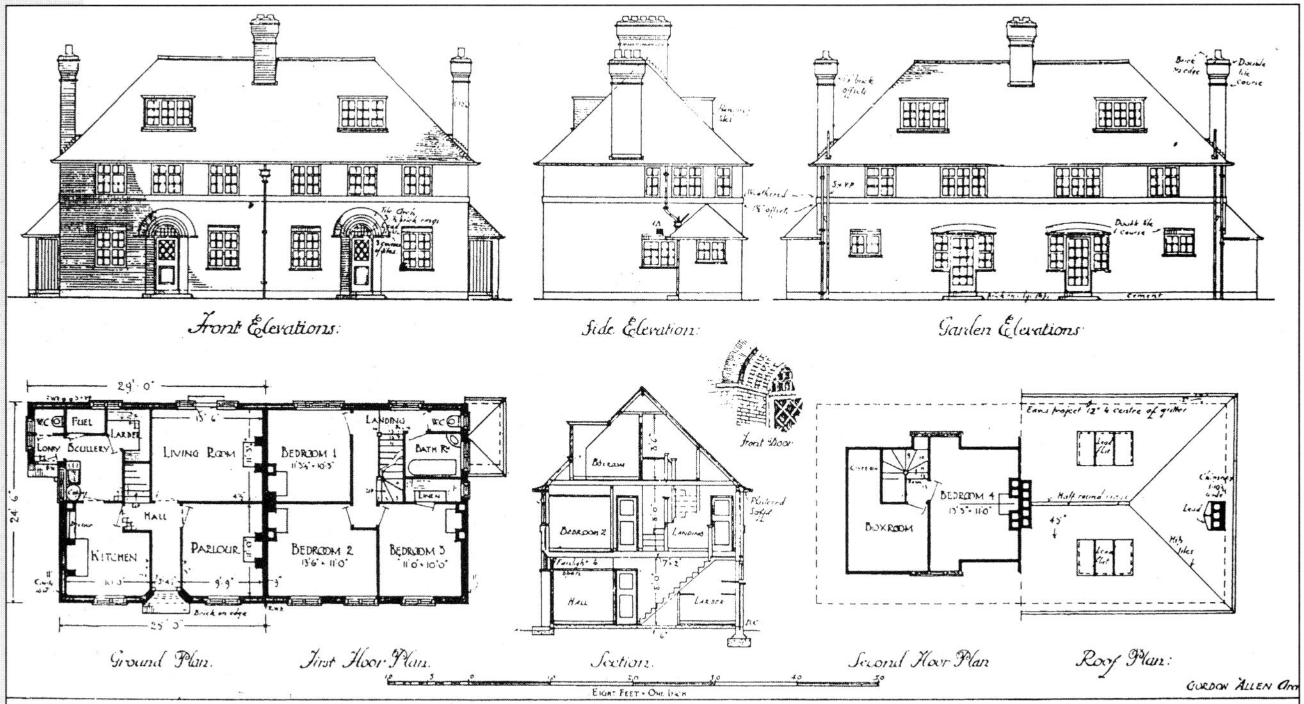

FIG. 17.—CRAYFORD GARDEN VILLAGE.

A number of these larger houses for Messrs. Vickers' staff were built at Crayford in 1916. The accommodation provided consists of two sitting-rooms, kitchen, scullery, and offices on the ground floor; three bedrooms, bathroom, etc., on the first floor; and a bedroom and large boxroom as attics. The walls are built with a continuous cavity, the facings being of dark purple brickwork. Red tiles were used for roofing. Over the front door is an arch of roofing tiles, as shown in the sketch.

Plans and elevations for houses on the Crayford Garden Village as designed by Gordon Allen and taken from his book The Cheap Cottage and Small House.

Welling

At the beginning of the twentieth century, East Wickham and Welling was a rural district. Housing was confined mainly to the High Street and along Belle Grove Road. There had been recent developments in the form of terraced houses along Upper Wickham Lane and in cul-de-sacs leading off it. The arrival of electric trams in 1903 stimulated similar developments mainly along the main road or in cul-de-sacs off it such

Hook Lane, Welling, c.1925. In the 1920s Welling was still predominantly rural in character as this picture illustrates. The view is taken from approximately the present junction with Churchfield Road looking south towards Little Danson Farm.

Welling

as Lewis, Granville, Bethel and Gipsy roads. Welling was turning into an important dormitory for Thameside workers, especially at Woolwich. The developments were almost exclusively working class; estates were built where small units of land were available close to the tram route on the margins of the Danson and Goldsmith estates. The First World War and the enormous increase of output of arms and munitions from Woolwich Arsenal had a very significant impact on Welling. To accommodate a huge influx of munitions workers a vast settlement of huts, generally known as the East Wickham Hutments, built in tidy rows, was set up south of St Michael's

Burnell Avenue, Welling, from Upper Wickham Lane towards Lovel Avenue, 1925, part of the Welling Council Housing Scheme. The total cost of the scheme was approximately £460,000 with the building costs of the 426 houses approximately £408,000.

Advertising hoardings for the Falconwood Park Estate on the Rochester Way, October 1933.

Church and also on the west side of Wickham Lane, south of Wickham Street and east of Lodge Lane near the border with Woolwich.

Another major development followed in the 1920s; the Welling Council Housing Scheme. As early as 1909 a housing inspection had indicated Welling as being the one area in the Bexley Urban District most in need of more housing. The War prevented any initiatives being taken. After the War, once it was satisfied that Government assistance would be forthcoming and following increasing local pressure, the Council

Falconwood: from woodland to suburbia

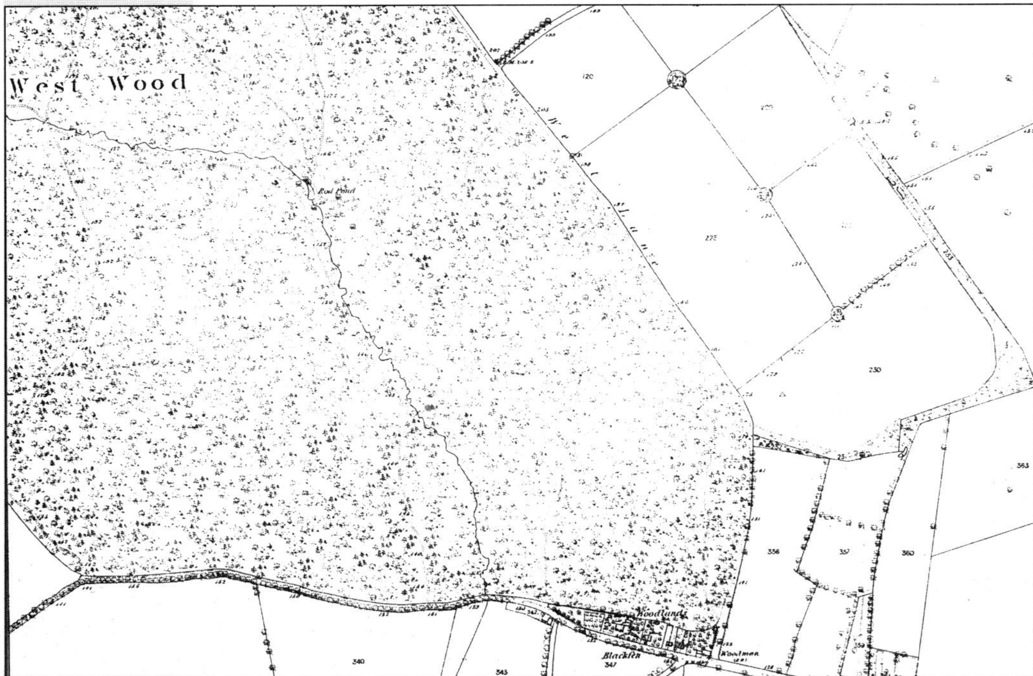

1862: *The ancient woodland of West Wood dominates. It was owned by Oxford University, Lords of the Manor of Bexley. Blackfen is a small hamlet on the Eltham to Bexley Road.*

1895: *West Wood has been cleared and replaced by Westwood Farm. Blackfen remains a hamlet.*

1933: *Westwood Farm is bisected by the recently-built Rochester Way. Development has started in the form of the unusually shaped Little Danson Estate and ribbon development along the Blackfen Road.*

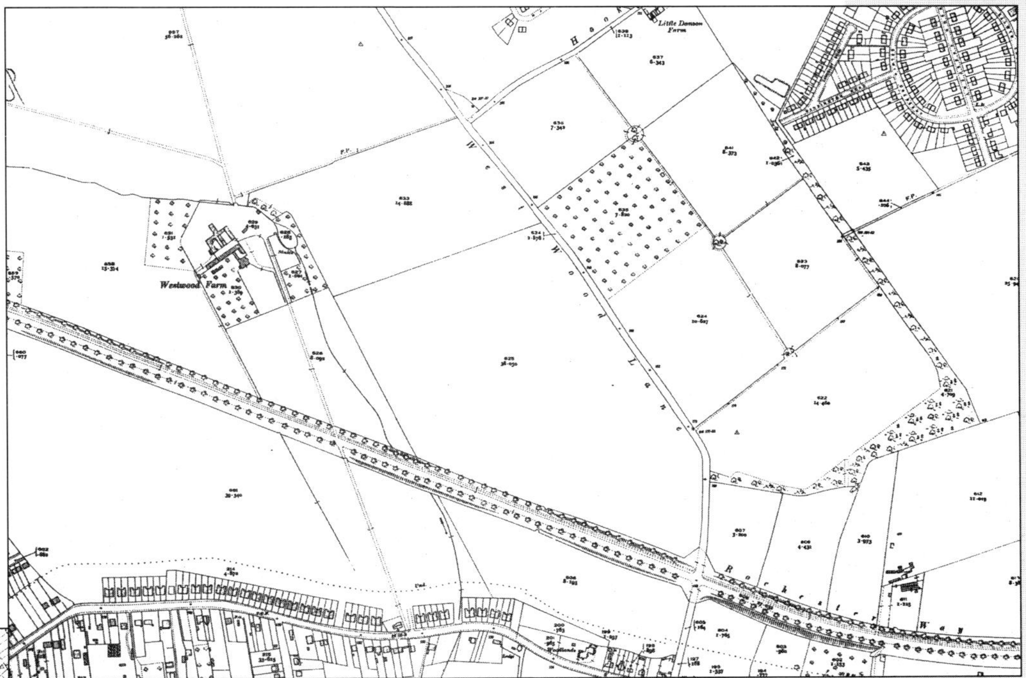

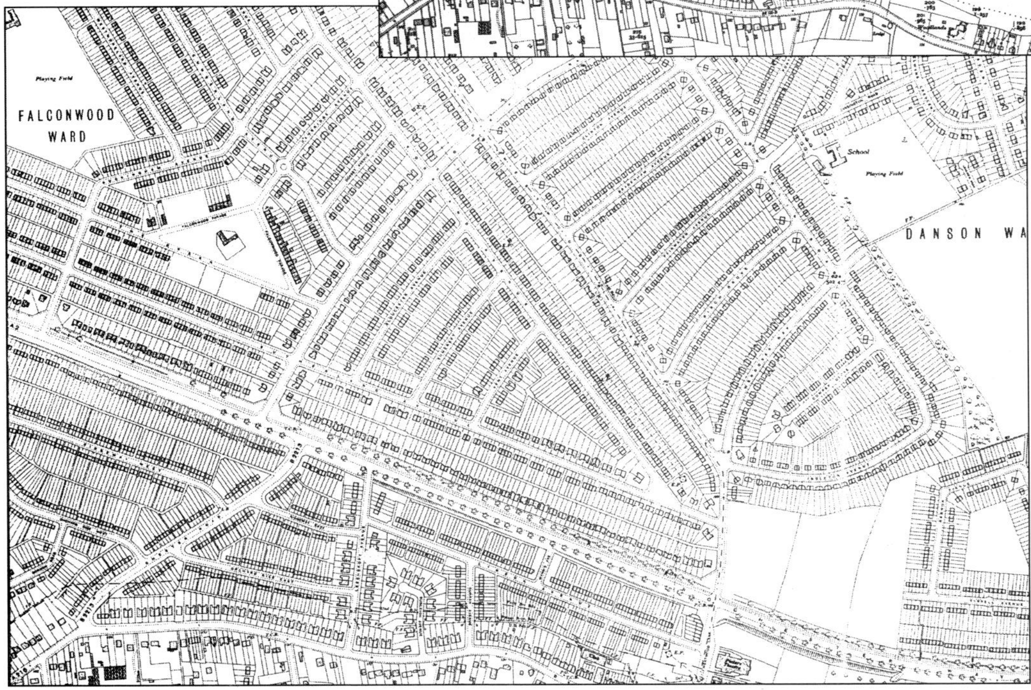

1936: *Westwood Farm has disappeared under a sea of housing: New Ideal Homesteads' Falconwood Park Estate. Virtually the only open spaces remaining are school playing fields and the western part of Danson Park.*

Welling

borrowed £400,000 in 1920 to undertake the large Welling Housing Scheme consisting of 426 houses. The scheme was completed in 1926. The layout was an enlightened one making very good use of the shape of the site.

Private development followed soon after. To the west of the council estate, private estate building could only occur because access to main water pipes and sewers were made possible by Council extension of these to serve their own Welling estate. Stevens' and Norman's estates mainly of modest semi-detached houses filled the space between Wickham Street and Central Avenue. To the south the break-up of the Danson Estate led to the building of the Little Danson Estate with its

Westmoreland and (right) Sutherland Avenues c.1934, part of New Ideal Homesteads' Falconwood Park Estate. The houses shown are type 'K' houses which sold for £550. The absence of trees (and the presence of the pylon) and the length and straightness of the roads creates an austere appearance.

distinctive circular Selwyn Crescent. Fortunately, the great central parkland was retained as one large unit of 222 acres. Thanks to the forethought and insistence of the Clerk to the Council, this was purchased and remains one of the largest parks in Greater London.

In the early 1930s the Bellegrove Park Building Estate was developed to the configuration of Bellegrove Park, a small country seat on the southern side of Bellegrove Road.

The Green, Falconwood, c.1939. The Green served as a focal point for the Falconwood Park Estate with its attractive mock-tudor shops and play-park. It occupies the site of Westwood Farm. The retention of the trees greatly enhances the scene.

Redevelopment of Welling High Street, 1930. The old cottages are making way for a new Co-op store.

Welling

By the mid-1930s the urban landscape of Welling was completely transformed by the huge estates of New Ideal Homesteads' Falconwood Park on Westwood Farm and the Stevens estates in the north-east of Welling. Between them these two firms built 5,000 houses from 1930 to 1936 adding 18,000 to the population of Welling. Shopping developments in the vicinity of Welling Corner and the High Street together with smaller shopping parades on the large estates, school, churches and open spaces completed the transformation. The whole district became known as Welling and what was left of the old hamlet of East Wickham became a relic feature eclipsed by twentieth century development.

Aerial view of the Falconwood Park Estate nearing completion, 1934.

Bexley in the 1930s

At the beginning of the 1930s, in spite of Victorian development Bexley Village was still a village surrounded by countryside.

In the 1920s there had been some change with small council-house estates in Hartford Road and Victoria Road (as the southern part of Albert Road was then known), and the opening of the

Suggested development scheme (not adopted) for the Blendon Hall Estate from the sales particulars of 1929. The eventual scheme was substantially different and Blendon Hall itself was demolished. The lakes survived into the post-war period but have now been drained and built upon.

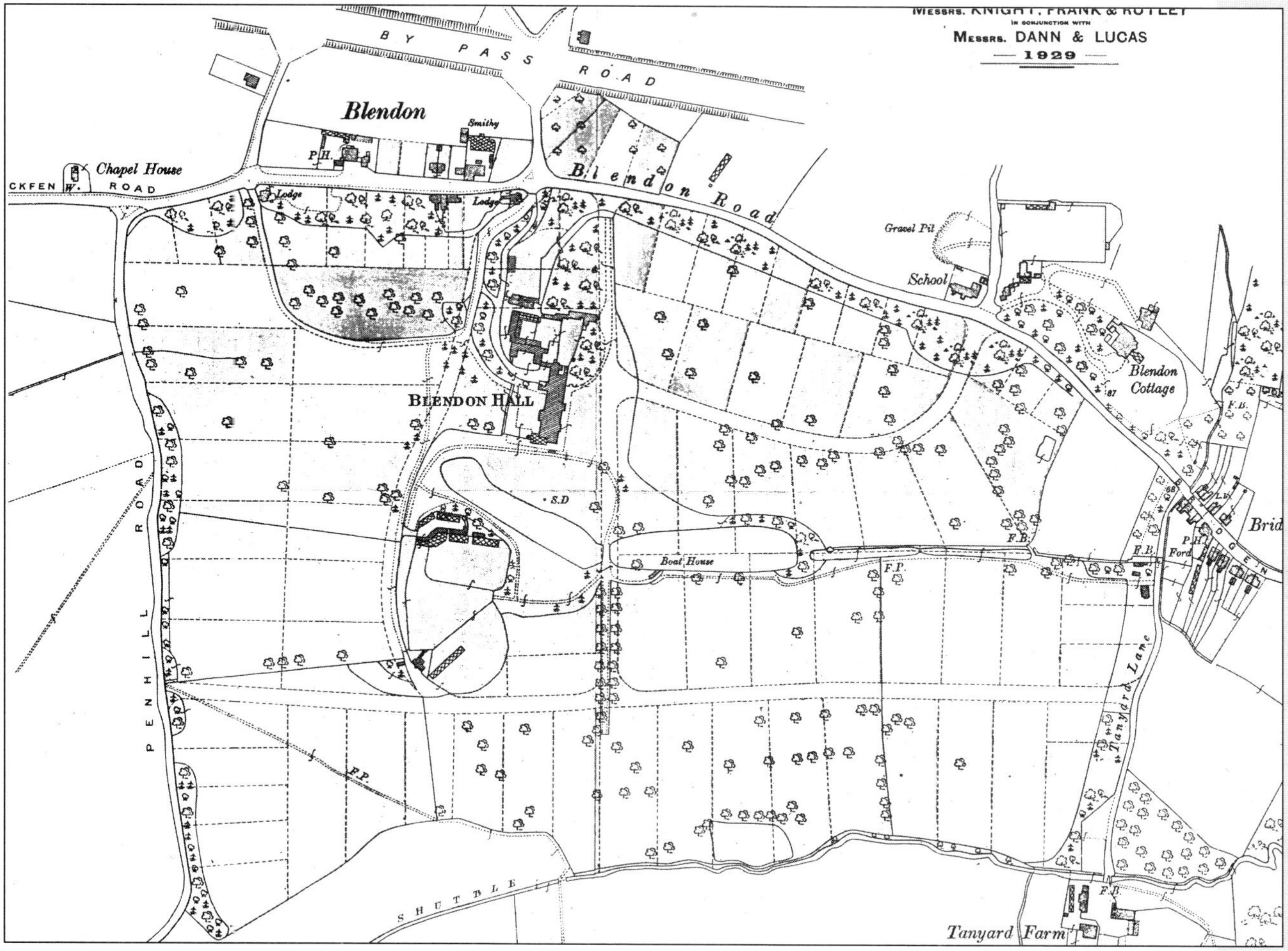

Bexley in the 1930s

Rochester Way and the building of the "Black Prince", a smart new mock-Tudor road house on the site of Bourne Place. By the early 1930s ribbon development had occurred along Upton Road, Parkhill Road, North Cray Road and Vicarage Road. By the middle of the decade the village was under threat as the large landed estates that surrounded it were broken up and developed. To the west Bridgen Place was the first to go with a development of semi-detached houses in Arbuthnot Lane. This was followed by the Blendon Hall Estate, purchased for development by D C Bowyer, and Tanyard and Hurst Farms, part of the Vansittart Estate, which were developed by New Ideal Homesteads as Albany Park.

Upton Road, Bexley, looking north, in the 1930s; an example of ribbon development along the old road.

A team of builders at Blendon Drive, c.1934-5.

Building the Glenhurst Estate Bexley, 1938. This estate was built on a field in between Hurst Road and the railway line.

Bexley in the 1930s

On the edge of the village itself, the Glenhurst Estate was developed on a large field on the south side of Hurst Road, part of Oxford University's Bexley Estate, separated from its Upper College Farm by the Railway. To the east there was further development at Baldwyn's Park and Coldblow. However, to the north east, Bexley Urban District Council in conjunction with the

Hurst Road, Glenhurst Estate 1938. The gates on the left-hand side lead to large Victorian Villas. The impending loss of their views across the Cray Valley must have been a source of great consternation to their occupants.

Greater London Regional Planning Committee was able to obtain a grant with which to acquire a large part of the Hall Place Estate as part of the "Green Belt Girdle" for Greater London: 62 acres were purchased for £25,000 in 1935 and in 1938, 40 acres of the neighbouring Halcot Estate for £20,410.

Houses being built on the Rochester Way, 1938; looking east towards Gravel Hill. The Rochester Way was opened in 1928. By the end of the 1930s it was lined with houses virtually the whole distance between Falconwood and Bexley.

Bexley in the 1930s

The demolition of Blendon Hall, 1934.

Bexleyheath, Barnehurst and Bostall in the 1930s

At the outset of the 1930s the town of Bexleyheath was still concentrated along or close to the main road of Crook Log/The Broadway/Watling Street. To the north especially, the picture was extremely rural with nurseries and fields stretching away to Belvedere with the odd terrace of farm labourers' cottages being the only form of habitation. The Bexleyheath railway line, opened in 1895, had not yet led to large scale development; in fact to the contrary, it had somewhat stimulated Bexleyheath as a market gardening area.

"Harvest", Long Lane, 1932. The southern side of Long Lane was already developed; the houses can be seen beyond the hedge. The northern side was soon to follow.

Pickford Lane, Bexleyheath, looking north, c.1931. Within a very short time this lane was widened and lined with semi-detached houses.

Bexleyheath, Barnehurst and Bostall in the 1930s

Mayplace Road East looking east, early 1930s. This view graphically shows the transformation from country lane to suburban street. The buildings of Mayplace Farm can ben seen in the distance.

By the end of the 1930s, however, this picture had changed most dramatically. The first of the major developments took place near Bexleyheath Station, the Brampton Park Estate, developed by D C Bowyer, with new roads being laid out between the old country lanes of Brampton Road and Pickford Lane. By the mid-1930s most of the south side of Long Lane had been developed and housing was moving in from the north with the development of Bostall and the Parsonage Farm Estate. To the east the new district of Barnehurst

Demolition of the farmhouse at Danson Farm at the junction of Danson and Bean Roads, 1930. In the background are newly-built detached houses with prestigious views across Danson Park.

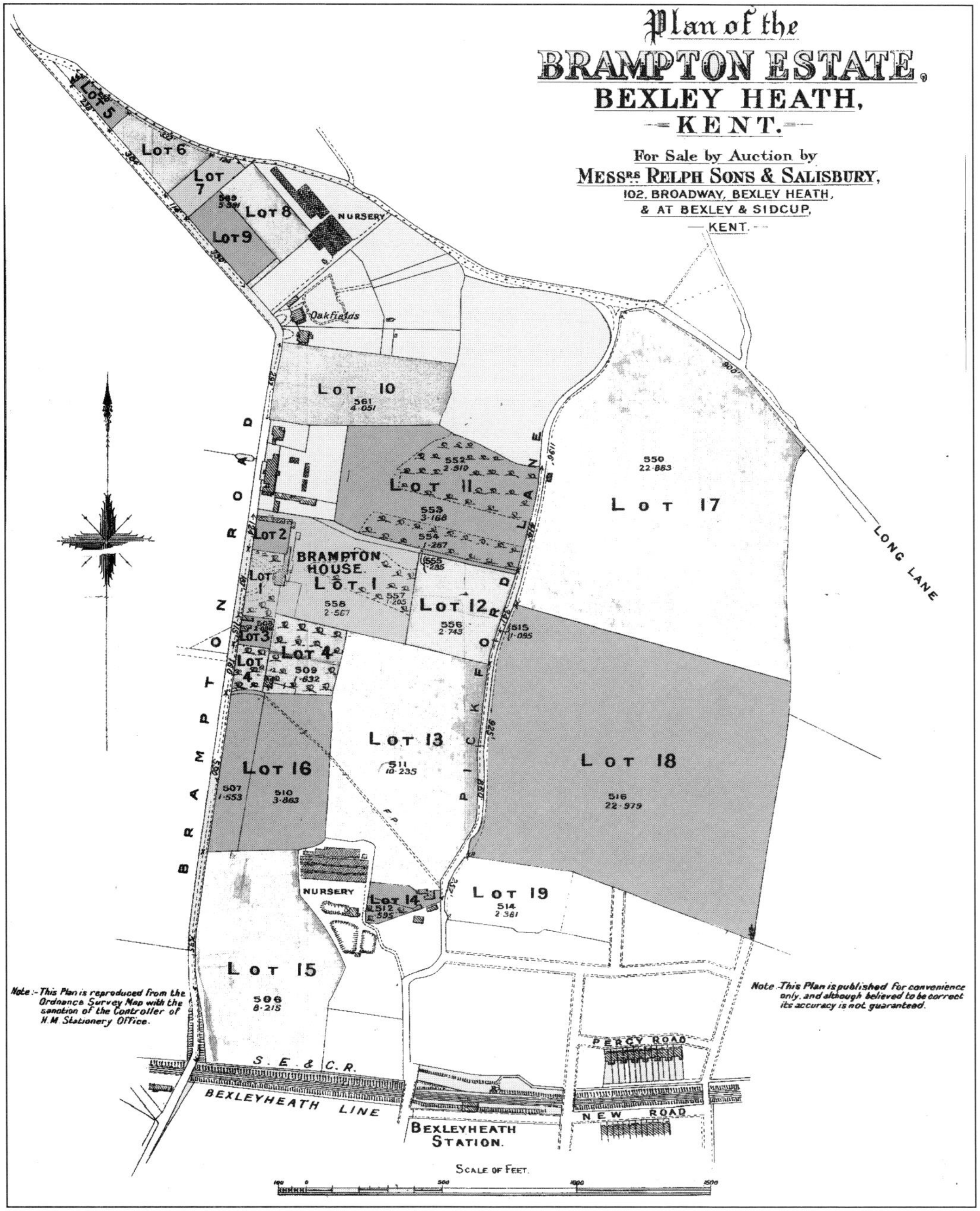

Plan of the Brampton Estate, Bexleyheath, 1926. This was mainly developed as bungalows by D. C. Bowyer.

Bexleyheath, Barnehurst and Bostall in the 1930s

A new parade of mock-tudor shops in Long Lane seen from the entrance to Sheldon's Farm, August 1935.

was emerging mainly within the Urban District of Crayford. Barnehurst was a name invented in 1895 for the station on the Bexleyheath line. Most of the development took place on the Mayplace Estate, with large developments by Ellingham's, Wedlock's and New Ideal Homesteads.

By the end of the 1930s the northern half of Bexleyheath had become one huge suburban area with Bexleyheath merging into Barnehurst, Northumberland Heath, Belvedere, Bostall and Welling; a seemingly endless sprawl of semi-detached houses and bungalows relieved only by parades of shops and the occasional open space.

Millfield Estate

Barnehurst.

Pleasant Suburb—Trams pass Estate—Near Shopping Centres

LAY-OUT PLAN.

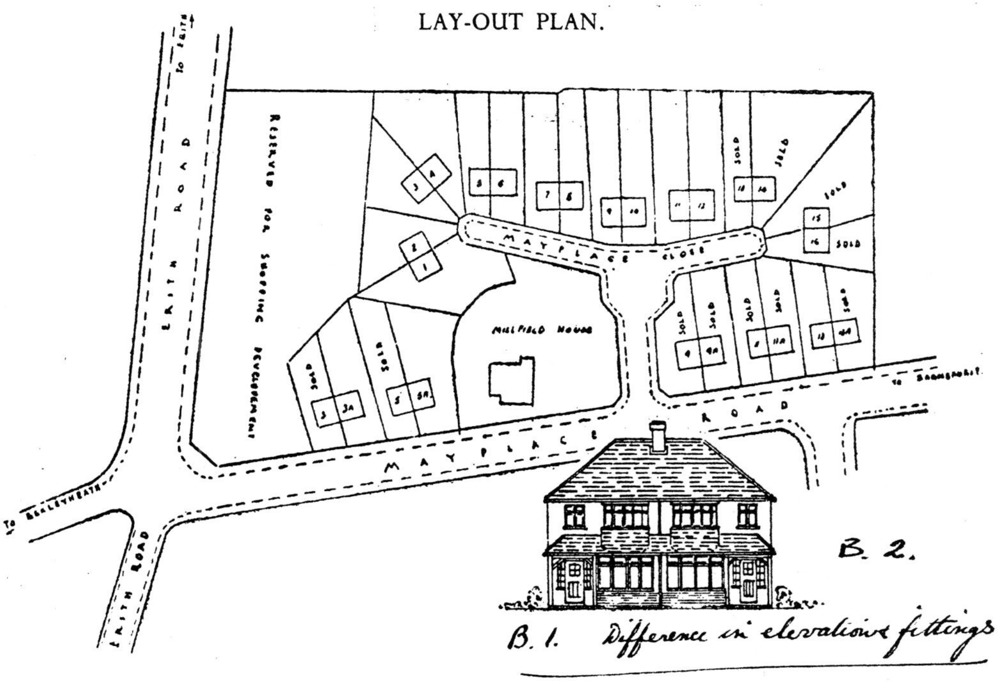

MILLFIELD, so named from its one time existence as the grounds of the old manor house which still stands at its centre, represents a first class suburban development. It is within very easy reach of the busy town of Bexleyheath although definitely removed from the hectic noise of the town itself and is connected by tram to both that place and Erith, yet another nearby town. Barnehurst is essentially a residential area but possesses several advanced shopping centres, a County Library Building, and an excellent Golf Club. The station, some ten minutes from Millfield, is on the Bexleyheath line from Charing Cross to Dartford and has a frequent Electric service to both London and Gravesend where connection for the coast is available. Crayford and the countryside is approximately one and a half miles away.

Sale particulars of the Millfield Estate, Mayplace Road, mid-30s. The estate takes its name from the windmill that used to stand on the site. Note that Barnehurst Library is featured as a selling point.

Bexleyheath, Barnehurst and Bostall in the 1930s

King Harold's Way, Bostall, 1931. These bungalows formed part of a large estate known initially as the St. Hilary Estate. They were built by Absoloms' on what had mainly been cabbage fields. The new houses preceded any amenities such as shops or schools and here even preceded the actual roads themselves, the building materials being delivered by a system of narrow gauge railways.

Chalet houses under construction in Avenue Road, Bexleyheath, 1932. The ultimate in 1930s suburban style, the "sunburst" gate is very much in evidence. Sadly, the fine trees were taken down in 1936.

On the south side of the Broadway there was building too, but the estates were on a much smaller scale and the houses generally of a higher class such as on Danson Road and Latham Road. The Mount Estate was further developed with small semi-detached housing along the south side of Mount Road and Grosvenor Road and Olron Crescent, the latter two roads designed to fit into

New Ideal Homesteads houses being built in Pelham Road, Bexleyheath, 1932. This is the east side from Woolwich Road. This small estate was built on part of Pelham Farm.

Bexleyheath, Barnehurst and Bostall in the 1930s

the roughly circular shape of an existing field. However, much of the Mount Estate survived house building by becoming Bexleyheath Golf Course. To the south the Rochester Way or Bexleyheath By-Pass as it was sometimes known, opened in 1926, effectively formed the boundary between Bexley and Bexleyheath and by the end of the thirties it was lined with houses on either side.

Redevelopment in the Broadway, 1932. Relph's estate agents and Dr Barnes' house (100, The Broadway), both mid-Victorian buildings are being demolished to make way for new shops. Ellingham's was among the leading builders in the district.

Sidcup and Blackfen

The Sidcup and Blackfen depicted in this section is very much the one of popular image; an area that developed principally in the 1930s, superficially suffering from the uniformity of suburban development. This is in fact only a very partial picture.

The 1909 map (see p. 78) shows that substantial areas remained undeveloped, especially around

The newly built Marechal Niel Parade on Main Road, Sidcup in 1937. The shops, successively a newsagents, grocers, greengrocers, butcher, hairdresser, baker and ironmonger, catered for the majority of the needs of local residents. Brunshaws were shortly to be taken over by Charringtons. Robins, the grocers, was the nearest to a chain with three shores locally. They remained in business until the early 1950s.

Sidcup and Blackfen

Crofton Avenue looking north on the Albany Park Estate. These are 'LB' type houses, new for £425.

Lamorbey and Halfway Street and stayed thus until the early 1930s. The period from then up to the outbreak of World War II was one of frantic development which saw the population increase from 12,355 in 1931 to 32,197 in 1951. The principal estates built were those of New Ideal Homesteads at Montrose Park, Marlborough Park and Albany Park, Smith's Hollies Estate and Leach's Burnt Oak Lane Estate. Several of Blackfen's new streets were developed as self-build properties. Factors that made this transformation possible were a combination of the local and national. Locally better transport became available through the electrification of the railway giving faster, more frequent and more affordable services and the building of the Sidcup By-Pass and Rochester Way. There was also an expansion of local manufacturing industry and a consequent demand for housing from skilled workers. Economically the depression enabled building societies to negotiate good deals with builders and consequently ask small deposits from borrowers. Technologically builders benefited from mass produced pre-fabricated fittings.

Harborough Avenue, Sidcup. This was part of the New Ideal Homesteads' estate built in 1935. It is a good example of higher density building; the apparently spacious pairs of 'semis' are in fact four, not two properties. These are 'LB' type properties which sold for £395 freehold, or 9/6d. (47½p) a week.

The Oval, Sidcup. This was part of the New Ideal Homesteads' Marlborough Park Estate. Shopping parades, though no other element of community infrastructure, were frequently included in residential developments. The Oval, built in 1933 was the largest and visually most striking example of this sort, in the district.

Sidcup and Blackfen

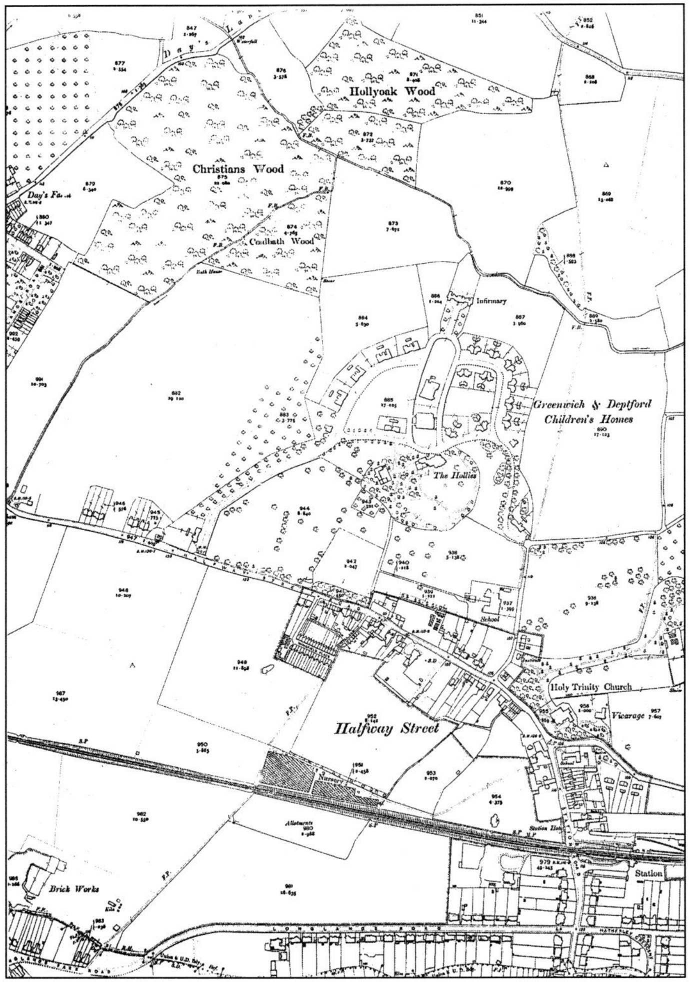

The 1909 and 1938 Ordnance Survey maps for the Halfway Street and Blackfen area. The extent of development is striking. Six separate developments occupied the land, New Ideal Homesteads' Marlborough Park Estate fanning south east from the Oval, Leach's Burnt Oak Lane Estate, Smith's Hollies Estate on Willersley Avenue and others centred on Days Lane, Old Farm Avenue and south of the railway in Longlands.

New Ideal Homesteads' publicity set the tone for much of the development; apparently stylish, spacious and semi-rural. Their use of colour and shape was alluring to the point of being brash and raised established residents' fears of what was to come. The cover of this book is based on their design for the Albany Park Estate brochure. Their fears were not based on the visual impact the hundreds of new properties would have; bland monotony of restrained mock Tudoring was presumably far more acceptable to incomers and locals alike than anything remotely progressive. Rather it was the former's perceived social class that caused anxiety as builders, particularly New

Ideal Homesteads, aimed their new properties at the very bottom of the market. Their publicity stressed low mortgage repayments and ease of purchase as much as efficiently-designed internal features and the possibility of installing prestigious high-tech labour-saving devices. New Ideal Homesteads judged their market perfectly and their estates attracted a rapid influx of moderately paid workers from Thameside industries and aspirant young City clerks, typically formerly resident in the declining inner suburbs.

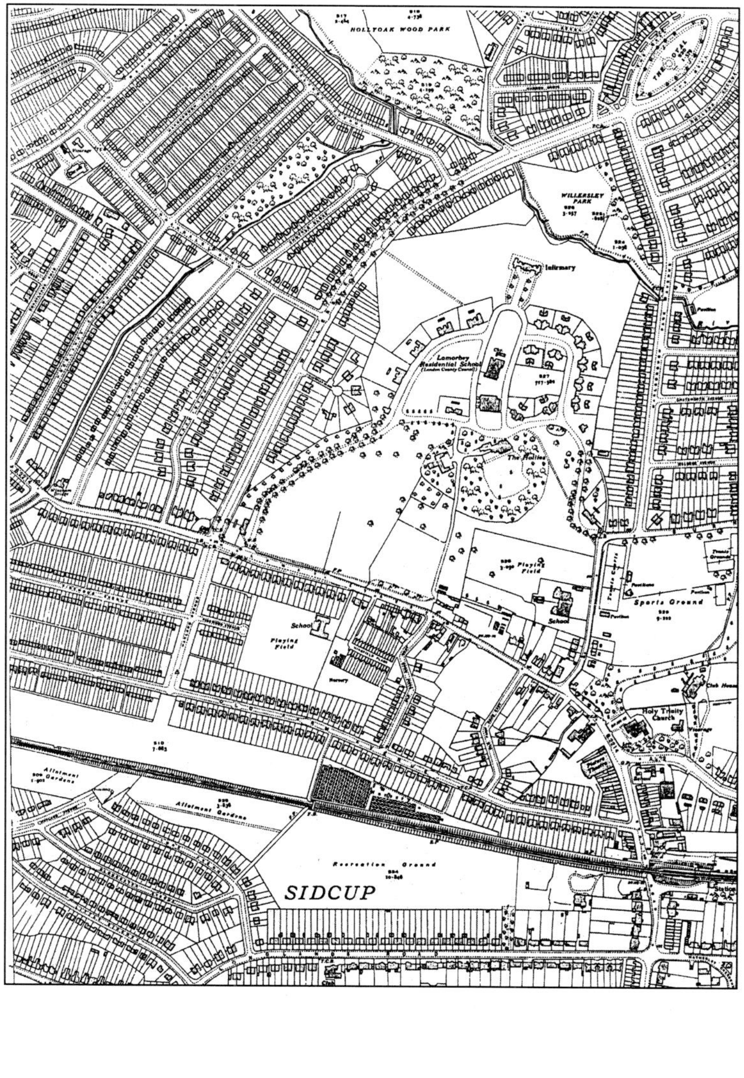

Sidcup and Blackfen

This aerial view of 1934 neatly shows many aspects of 1930s development. It looks north across Hurst Road and shows contrasting developments by New Ideal Homesteads at Albany Park to the south (middleground) and Bowyers more upmarket and steadily paced development at Blendon Hall. The River Shuttle running west-east across the view is in large part the boundary between them. The view shows New Ideal Homesteads' approach of very rapid and systematic building and their practice of taking on awkward shaped sites and tolerating areas of waste land within the developments such as the triangle inside Hurst Road and Shirley and Howard Avenues. Blendon Hall to the north still stands. Bowyer had hoped to retain it for use as a private school but due to insufficient middle income families the idea failed. The house was demolished and the site developed. The Rochester Way, a powerful catalyst in the development process, runs across the north east (top right) corner of the photograph.

The Sidcup By-Pass in 1936. The old cottages still stand dwarfed by an elevated roundabout at the A20, A222 junction.

They moved to a landscape that, if far from the permanently maintained, undisfigured charming countryside that New Ideal Homesteads promised (and destroyed), was visually inoffensive and into properties that provided immediate attractions of modern amenities powered by electricity, the space (in bedrooms and garden) to accommodate a growing family and even a garage. Much of the advertising had been unashamedly aimed at wives. New Ideal Homesteads proclaimed their's was "the house designed by the woman for the woman", and thereby strengthening the woman's position within the domestic partnership at least at the time of purchase. Ironically, suburbanisation traditionalised the wife's role in the marriage relationship more than ever. Absent husbands, geographical isolation from parents and in-laws, young children and a young population all made the home the overwhelming focus of activity.

If New Ideal Homesteads' achievements may have offended the day's progressive designers, the

Sidcup and Blackfen

The Sidcup By-Pass in 1935. As well as providing a Sunday afternoon spectacle, the road had profound effects on the timing of suburban development.

area's social elite and the local authorities' ambitions for low housing densities (Bexley Council proposed eight properties per acre, New Ideal Homesteads built at almost double that) they rarely offended the building control officers. This is commendable given the scale and speed of the operation as for example the Hurst Road and Albany Park Estates saw the building of 2,500 houses in two years.

Such considerations were irrelevant to newcomers such as Mrs Kar, who moved into the area in 1933. Apprehensive as to the reception she would receive she recalled "when we came into Sidcup Hill at first we thought they were snobs" but this was outweighed by the overall verdict of the area as a "great advantage..... wonderful, lovely country, lovely houses and... so cheap".

The co-existence of the rural and the urban on Thamesmead is as real today as during the building of Thamesmead South in 1970. Here swans find a home on what is to become South Mere. Today the combination of still-undeveloped wild areas, planned nature parks as at Tump 53 and extensive watercourses provide the habitat for a large variety of birds.

The Thamesmead depicted in this section shows its urban face although it is in reality a landscape of great variety. Alongside housing developments of slab concrete are small scale ones evocative of a vernacular village style, industrial and shopping centres, and large areas yet undeveloped all interspersed with a network of footpaths and an imaginative use of artificial watercourses.

Thamesmead

Work under way on Thamesmead South in early 1969. Although constructed from pre-cast concrete slabs, the builders were keen to emphasise that the design was different to that of Ronan Point, the tower block that collapsed the previous year.

Thamesmead is unique in London, being a planned new town built on the back of post war housing needs, the optimism and the buoyancy of 1960s and 1970s economic success and the ethos of centrally-planned large-scale public developments.

Thamesmead was named after widespread consultation by the Greater London Council and Greenwich and Bexley Councils. The name adopted in 1967 was suggested to the Kentish Times by Barnehurst resident, Mr Anthony Walton.

Erith Observer & Kentish Times

No. 5098–92nd Year | TEL. ERITH 35741 | FRIDAY, JANUARY 20, 1967 | LARGEST NETT SALE | 28 PAGES–5d.

We will call it THAMESMEAD Committee decide

K.T. READER NAMES NEW TOWN

Labourer crushed to death

A SWANLEY labourer was crushed to death at an Erith building site on Saturday, just days before his wife was expecting their third child.

Mr. Absolom Rye, aged 32, of 37, Lime-road, Swanley, was killed when an unmanned lion dumper truck ran forward and fell into a pit in which he was working. No one saw the accident at the Riverviey Estate building site, at Valley-road.

Mr. Rye had worked for W. E. G. Spiller, contractor, of Abbotts-close, Swanley, for eight years.

Mr. Spiller said this week: "Mr. Rye was working in a 10ft. deep trench and another man parked the truck about 85ft. away on a slope when he went to make the tea.

TRUCK IN PIT

"He returned three minutes later and saw the truck in the pit. The police, fire brigade and ambulance were called at once.

"It is very unfortunate that the foreman should have been called away to the telephone just before this happened," he said.

Erith firemen used hydraulic jacks and blocks to lift the dumper from the trapped man. Mr. Rye was rushed to St. Nicholas' Hospital, Plumstead, but was dead on arrival.

FOURTH TRAGEDY

This was the fourth tragedy to hit the Rye family in just over a year. In that time, Mr. Rye's mother and aunt died and his cousin, Philip, was drowned at Maidstone.

Mr. Rye was born in Swanley and lived there all his life apart from his National Service in Germany from 1957 to 1959. He leaves a wife, Mavis, aged 28, and two children

Barnehurst man is winner from 565 entries

THAMESMEAD—the name chosen by the Woolwich-Erith Development Sub-Committee for the 1,300-acre riverside project—was submitted by a reader who took part in the "Kentish Times" "Name the New Town" competition.

The sub-committee, consisting of members of the G.L.C. and Greenwich and Bexley Councils, enlisted the help of the public in the difficult task of finding an acceptable name for the project.

No fewer than 565 names were received through the Press, by telephone and letter to County Hall and to the two Town Halls.

The largest contribution resulted from the competition organised by the "Kentish Times," and included the winning entry, "Thamesmead," by Mr. Anthony Walton, of 32, Edendale-road, Barnehurst.

THE RUNNER-UP

The runner-up was Mrs. K. E. Walter, of 26, Beacon-road, Hither Green, a reader of the *South East London Mercury* who, in a list of 22 suggestions, included "Thamesmeade"—one additional letter.

Mr. Walton went to County Hall, Westminster, on Tuesday where he received the *Kentish Times* prize of £20 from Sir William Fiske, Leader of the G.L.C. and chairman of the sub-committee.

Making the presentation, Sir William congratulated the *Kentish Times* for organising the competition and thanked all those who had submitted entries.

He said that when the revised master plan was published in March he would autograph a copy of the brochure and present it to Mr. Walton.

THE PRESENTATION

Mr. J. S. Massey, Editor-in-Chief of the *Kentish Times* Series, thanked Sir William for making the presentation and also Mr. Peter Maxwell, Leader of Bexley Council, for

gestion should be used for such an important project."

Both he and his wife spent several hours thinking of a suitable name, and Mr. Walton was convinced that "Thames" should figure in their final suggestion.

REGULAR READER

A regular reader of the *Kentish Times*, Mr. Walton takes a keen interest in local affairs.

The word "Thames" formed part of 53 suggestions. Other suggested names ranged from "Abberkh" to "Wrothness" and included "Churchill Town," "Elizabeth," Gallions," "Lesnes Town," "Meridian," "New Woolerton," "Picardy" and "Winston Green."

"Thamesmead" will eventually provide home for 60,000 Londoners, the site is bounded by the Thames for three miles and is twice the combined size of Hyde Park and Kensington Gardens. Part of it is in Bexley and part in Greenwich.

A revised master plan is expected to be published in March before being submitted to the Minister of Housing and Local Government.

A contract worth nearly £3,000,000 was awarded in November, 1966, to Holland and Hannen and Cubitts (Southern), Ltd., to build the first 4,000 homes.

Mr. Anthony Walton (second from the right), of 12, Edendale-road, Barnehurst, who won the "Kentish Times" competition for naming the new town to be built on the Woolwich Arsenal / Erith Marshes site, is pictured at County Hall, London, on Tuesday, after receiving his prize, a cheque for £26, from Sir William Fiske, Leader of the G.L.C. On the extreme right is Councillor Peter Maxwell, Leader of Bexley Council, and on the left is Mr. J. S. Massey, Editor-in-Chief of the "Kentish Times" Series.—(K.T. Photo No. JZ/8432).

HOMELESS SOON, SAYS WIDOW

Plight of late Vicar's family

A VICAR'S widow told the "Kentish Times" this week that she and her two younger daughters will soon be homeless because Bexley Council will not help them.

She is 59-year-old Mrs. Winifred Jocelyn, widow of the Vicar of Christ Church, the Rev. Kenneth Jocelyn, who died in November.

Mrs. Jocelyn is still living at the Vicarage in Victoria-road, but her tenure actually expired five weeks after her husband's death.

She told the *Kentish Times* this week that possession of the Vicarage was urgently required by the Church authorities for work to be put in hand so that a new Vicar can be appointed.

Mrs. Jocelyn said she had not enough money to buy a new home. As she was nearing retirement from teaching it was not easy to leave the area and change her job.

EMERGENCY

"As I have lived 11½ years in Erith, I naturally applied to the Housing Office to be considered as a person about to be evicted and needing housing in an emergency," she went on.

"No suggestion was ever made to me that I was not eligible, but after a silence of two months, my application was turned down and I was merely put on a waiting list. What good is that to me?"

When she protested, Mrs. Jocelyn claims, the Housing Manager replied that they were free, in an almshouse for the widows of clergymen. At the moment she was ineligible.

"What am I to do? The Housing Manager has made it quite clear that if I refer myself to the Housing Office I shall have to wait at least 12 months before anything can be done for me.

"Meanwhile it seems as if my younger children and myself must move into furnished rooms and store or sell the furniture."

A spokesman for Rochester Diocesan Office said the Church had done all in its power to help Mrs. Jocelyn. She was receiving a pension from the Church, but he was unable to say when she would be required to leave the vicarage.

The Town Clerk of Bexley (Mr. Clive Dennis) told the *Kentish Times*: "Application for accommodation was made by Mrs. Jocelyn in the course of a long interview on November 15, approximately two weeks after the death of Mr. Jocelyn.

"DID NOT CONFORM"

"Mrs. Jocelyn was informed that this was a case that did not conform to normal housing policy and on November 17 she was told in writing that the case would be submitted for consideration at a committee meeting on January 1 (the first meeting following the application).

JURY SLATE L.E.B. SAFETY MEASURES

Three breadwinners died by accident

MAYOR'S PLEA FOR LEPROSY SUFFERERS

THE Mayor of Bexley (Councillor K. J. Smith, J.P.) writes to the Editor:

"World Day for Leprosy Sufferers will be celebrated this year on Sunday, January 29. This day brings to the notice of a largely indifferent public the needs and suffering of the estimated 15,000,000 leprosy sufferers in the world today.

"Leprosy can be cured. Drugs can control the disease, and physiotherapy and surgery can either prevent or

GANG'S

Head master's

Thamesmead

The London County Council which planned the scheme identified the site in the late 1950s. It combined the advantages of proximity to London, relative lack of development, and available land already controlled by public bodies. The land in question belonged to the Ministry of Defence's huge armaments complex, the Woolwich Arsenal, which was in the process of relocation and contraction. Adjacent to it was a vacant site owned by the L.C.C. in connection with the sewage works at Crossness. These factors also suggest some of the site's disadvantages. As well as pollution (land and airborne) the site was a low marsh, (much is below the high tide level) with a high water table. These problems are compounded by the area's geology, its geographical isolation and poor transport infrastructure.

A "complete environment" was planned with a balance of housing, educational, commercial and recreational facilities. It was to accommodate at least 60,000 and provide employment for 16,000. Work commenced in Thamesmead South in 1967 with the building of the now unfashionably-styled monolithical concrete tower and deck-access blocks. Thamesmead Central was developed from 1971 and contains the first part of the town centre and the Pumping Station at Thamesmere, which regulates the intricate network of drainage canals and lakes. The residential Thamesmead North started in 1977 and the industrial Thamesmead East in 1979.

Thamesmead today provokes strong reactions both to its townscape and perceived social problems. The latter have been exaggerated and highlighted by the popular media and ironically by the area being used as a location for a film which cannot now be shown in the UK, based on Anthony Burgess' 'A Clockwork Orange'. Its problems are statistically no worse than much of London.

It is now under the management of Thamesmead Town, a private company, which continues the development aiming for completion in c. 2010 with a final population of 40,000.

Post-war developments

Since the end of the war development and re-development has continued right across the Borough, but the scale and speed of change of the 1930s has of course never been seen again.

In the immediate post-war years in addition to the rebuilding necessitated by bombing, work continued on completing estates interrupted by the war such as Royal Park Estate at Albany Park. Many of the larger developments since the war have been council estates, notably by the Erith Borough Council and the Crayford Urban District Council, but also in the south of the Borough such as the Chislehurst and Sidcup Urban District Council's Bedensfield Estate at North Cray and Bexley London Borough's estates at Footscray.

Chislehurst and Sidcup Urban District Council's Bedensfield Estate, North Cray. This estate on the very edge of suburbia was completed in 1961. It was imaginatively designed making effective use of small greens and closes. The estate was made up of 485 dwellings in a mixture of houses and flats.

Post-war developments

Steel-framed houses being erected in Halcot Avenue, Bexleyheath by the Crayford Urban District Council, March 1947.

Crayford Urban District Council's Arthur Street housing development, Slade Green, March 1962. This mixed high-density scheme provided 265 dwellings.

Post-war developments

Development of the Hurst Farm Estate, May 1952. Hurst Farm with its twin oast houses had somehow survived the suburban onslaught of the 1930s. This imaginatively laid out housing scheme was built by Bexley Borough Council.

Post-war developments

New housing at the junction of Parkhill and Parkhurst Roads, March 1962. These houses replaced one large Victorian one - Marl House (see pp. 30-31). In the distance is Tower House also now demolished for redevelopment.

Private development has largely been limited to relatively small scale developments often on odd pieces of land left out of 1930s developments for one reason or another. Single houses have been built in the gardens of corner plots and cul-de-sacs pushed through between houses with large back gardens. Since the 1960s re-development of Victorian parts of the Borough has been commonplace, most notably in Upper Belvedere, Erith, Bexley and Sidcup with large Victorian houses making way for blocks of flats, maisonettes or sheltered accommodation.

Post-war developments

The changing face of Erith. In the 1980s some of Erith's redundant industrial areas gave way to housing. These are in the "pseudo-warehouse" style, which remains popular for riverside developments such as this.

Pressure on undeveloped land is great. In the last 20 years there have been several (unsuccessful) schemes, for example, to develop the Russell Stoneham Estate on Crayford Marshes. In the 1980s and 1990s controversy has surrounded the building of houses on open spaces such as at The Hollies, Sidcup and on school playing fields.

Select Bibliography

The research for this book has been undertaken using the extensive collections, both published and archival, of the Bexley Local Studies Centre at Hall Place. The following works have been particularly useful.

Allen, Gordan **The cheap cottage and small house,** Batsford, 1919.

Carr, M C **The development and character of a metropolitan suburb: Bexley, Kent** in Thompson, FML (ed) **The rise of suburbia,** Leicester University Press, 1982.

Hamilton, J E **The industries of Crayford,** Bexley Libraries and Museums, 1980.

Nunns, B N **A short history of Sidcup** in Turner, J **Seven gardens for Catherine,** Cassells, 1968.

Prichard, John **A history of Erith** parts 1-5, Bexley Libraries and Museums, 1976-1994.

Mercer, John **The Sidcup story,** Bexley Libraries and Museums, 1988.

Quiney, Anthony **House and home,** BBC Publications, 1986.

Shaw, J C M **The Bexleyheath phenomenon,** Bexley Libraries and Museums, 1983.

Spurgeon, Darrell **Discover Bexley and Sidcup,** Greenwich Guide-Books, 1993.

Spurgeon, Darrell **Discover Crayford and Erith,** Greenwich Guide-Books, 1995.

Tester, P J **Bexley village,** Bexley Libraries and Museums, 1987.

Index

Index